Mothers Against Drunk Driving

This special edition of the "Food Writers' Favorites: Cookies" benefits MADD. Before enjoying the many recipes that follow, please take a few minutes to read over the prefatory material. It explains the steps you can take to prevent drunk driving, provides a history of MADD, and recaps many of the programs and services available through the organization. After reading these pages, MADD hopes you will take a more active part in making the roads safer for all of us.

"THE MISSION OF MOTHERS AGAINST DRUNK DRIVING IS TO STOP DRUNK DRIVING AND TO SUPPORT VICTIMS OF THIS VIOLENT CRIME."

Two of every five Americans will be involved in an alcohol-related crash in their lifetime. In 1989, an estimated 22,415 people were killed and 345,000 injured as the result of alcohol- and other drug-impaired driving crashes. Through your support and involvement, we can eliminate this senseless crime.

HOW CAN YOU HELP PREVENT DRUNK DRIVING?

Drunk driving is a crime. There are several ways you can help reduce the tragic results of alcohol- and other drug-impaired driving.

- Do not refer to incidents caused by alcohol- and other drug-impaired drivers as "accidents." These crashes are not accidental because they result from two clear choices: (1) to consume alcohol or use other drugs; and (2) to drive.

- Never drink and drive and never allow a friend to drink and drive.

- Speak out against alcohol- and other drug-impaired driving in your community.

- Support legislation to reform drunk driving laws. Contact your local, county, state and federal officials to show your interest and support.

- Follow drunk driving cases from the initial report by the arresting officer through the judicial process in your community or county. Is the process working? Report what you find to the media, your legislators and state or local MADD officials.

- Designate a driver *BEFORE* you leave the house if your outing involves drinking. And, encourage your friends to always do the same.

- Start educating your children early with the truth about alcohol and other drugs.

- Refuse to serve alcohol to any young person until he or she is 21 years of age. It's the law.

1

- Remember that alcohol — including beer, wine, wine coolers and liquor — is a drug.
- Understand that your ability to think clearly and react appropriately can be impaired by alcohol and other drugs long before you become visibly intoxicated.
- Remember that cold showers, coffee or exercise do not lower the level of intoxication. Only time does that — alcohol burns off much more slowly than it is consumed.
- Report suspected drunk drivers promptly to the police.

The National Highway Traffic Safety Administration offers several ways to identify suspected drunk drivers. Alcohol- and other drug-impaired drivers frequently:

- Follow other vehicles too closely or drive with their headlights off at night;
- Drink in the vehicle or drive with the face close to the windshield;
- Weave or zig-zag across the road or drive into opposing traffic;
- Drive slower than 10 m.p.h. below the speed limit;
- Use turn signals that are inconsistent with driving actions or stop in a traffic lane.

If you see a suspected drunk driver, **DO NOT:**

- Attempt to stop the vehicle, or to follow it if the driver is exceeding the posted speed limit;
- Disregard traffic signals if you are following the vehicle;
- Follow the vehicle too closely — the driver may stop suddenly;
- Attempt to detain the drunk driver if he or she stops.

But, you **SHOULD** *call the nearest law enforcement agency and:*

- Tell them you want to report a drunk driver;
- Give the exact location (identify the street or road and direction in which the vehicle is traveling);
- Give a description of the vehicle (license plate number, color, make, model);
- Describe how the vehicle is being driven.

THE HISTORY OF MADD

MADD was founded in California in 1980. An aggressive grassroots campaign resulted in California passing the toughest drunk driving laws in the country at that time.

This astounding success was only the beginning. MADD soon grew into a nationwide organization with almost 3,000,000 members and supporters. Today, thousands of concerned citizens are involved in more than 400 chapters in the United States with affiliates in Canada, Australia, New Zealand, and Great Britain. MADD is made up of men and women of all ages who share a common concern for safety on our roads.

Since MADD's founding in 1980, more than 1,200 anti-drunk driving laws have been enacted nationwide. The rights of victims and survivors of alcohol- and other drug-related crashes are now viewed more equitably in a criminal justice system that only a few years ago paid little attention to them.

MADD PROGRAMS

Community Programs
MADD develops programs throughout the year to promote public awareness and raise the nation's consciousness about the dangers of alcohol- and other drug-impaired driving.

PROJECT RED RIBBON was created by MADD in 1986 to change the meaning of "tie one on." MADD asks drivers to tie a red ribbon to a visible location on their vehicles between Thanksgiving and New Year's Day to show their commitment to drive safe and sober throughout the year. Please take part in this simple but effective program during the holiday season.

Keep It a Safe Summer (K.I.S.S.) Campaign spreads the word that summer months can be the most dangerous. The *Family Vacation Pack* is filled with safety tips and activities for the entire family. Help MADD keep it a safe (and sober) summer on our nation's roads and waterways.

Designated Driver is a program with a simple point: if you choose to drink, bring along a friend who is not drinking to safely drive you home. You can help promote the program by always using a designated driver and offering to be the designated driver for your friends.

DRIVE FOR LIFE is an annual public awareness campaign with one compelling goal: to save lives by focusing attention on drunk driving during Labor Day weekend. MADD asks you to drive with your headlights on throughout *DRIVE FOR LIFE* Day (the Saturday before Labor Day) in memory of the 61 men, women and children killed each day by drunk drivers and to sign a pledge not to drink and drive.

Candlelight Vigils remind us of the thousands of loved ones killed or injured in drunk driving crashes. Please attend the *Candlelight Vigil of Remembrance and Hope* in your community to show your support for a less violent future.

Youth Programs
It is illegal for anyone under the age of 21 to be served or to consume alcohol in every state in the nation. Since the national minimum drinking age was implemented, the proportion of drivers under 21 involved in alcohol-related crashes has dramatically declined from 28% in 1982 to 17% in 1989.

Young people today receive many "mixed messages." MADD's message to this group is clear: drinking under the age of 21 is unacceptable and illegal. MADD has developed programs to educate young people how to avoid dangerous situations involving alcohol and other drugs.

Operation Prom/Graduation — TH!NK is a nationwide program designed to make prom and graduation nights memorable occasions, not memorials. They center on alcohol- and other drug-free celebrations for high school-age students. Please support *Operation Prom/Graduation* and *TH!NK* activities in your community.

MADD Poster/Essay Contest invites students in grades 1-12 to use their creative skills to deliver strong messages against drinking and driving. English- and Spanish-language entries are welcome and local first place entries compete nationally. Contact MADD's Youth Programs Department for information and this year's theme.

The MADD Student Library is published annually to provide information about the impact of alcohol and other drugs on young people. It includes statistics, articles on topics such as peer pressure, and a bibliography on resources for highway safety issues. Check your school library to be sure they have a current copy on file.

Friends Keep Friends Alive! is an educational comic book with an instructor's guide for use in grades 4-9. The comic book teaches children how to say "no" to drinking in both English and Spanish versions.

FREE FOR LIFE is a refusal skills program that teaches junior high students how to resist peer pressure to use alcohol and other drugs. The program relies on "peer education" techniques, and students themselves plan and lead class discussions.

PUBLIC POLICY AND LEGISLATIVE GOALS

During its 10th Anniversary in 1990, MADD renewed its focus on two primary goals: aiding the victims of alcohol- and other drug-related crashes and reducing the incidence of this type of impaired driving.

20 x 2000
Alcohol-related fatalities now account for approximately 50% of all traffic fatalities. MADD's goal is to reduce that number by an additional 20% by the year 2000. MADD urges you, and all levels of government, to support this effort by focusing on these five objectives.

Youth Issues: Reducing the number of young people involved in alcohol- and other drug-impaired driving incidents requires more than enacting a minimum drinking age of 21. Alcohol-free areas should be maintained around schools and during youth functions, young people must be educated about the hazards of alcohol and other drugs, appropriate penalties must be applied to adults who supply alcohol and other drugs to anyone under the age of 21, and youths who commit such offenses must be properly penalized.

4

Enforcement: Effective tools are available to enforce DWI laws. We must support the use of sobriety checkpoints, preliminary breath tests and passive alcohol sensors, a *per se* limit of an appropriate level such as .08, mandatory Blood Alcohol Content (BAC) testing when crashes result in injury or loss of life, and limits on open alcohol containers in vehicles.

Sanctions: Appropriate sanctions are effective deterrents to DWI crime. Sanctions against alcohol- and other drug-impaired driving that have proven to be effective include administrative license revocation and mandatory jail time for repeat offenders. Other approaches that may reduce repeat offenses include license plate/vehicle confiscation, increasingly severe penalties for subsequent convictions, and elimination of charge reduction negotiations. Minimum-security facilities to incarcerate DWI offenders could provide education and treatment. DWI offenses involving death or serious injury, or when the driver leaves the scene of such a crash, should be felonies and receive penalties in accordance with the seriousness of the crime. Improvement in monitoring DWI offenses from the time of arrest through the disposition of the case in court is necessary to identify and better deal with multiple offenders. This would also provide better documentation of the DWI problem and effective solutions that are being implemented on a state and national basis.

Self-Sufficient Programs: MADD advocates channeling DWI fines, fees and other assessments, including user fees such as alcohol excise taxes, to ensure consistent, long term funding for comprehensive anti-drunk driving law enforcement.

Responsible Marketing and Service of Alcohol: Increased responsibility in the marketing and serving of alcoholic beverages is imperative. MADD does not call for legislated limits on beverage advertising but strongly urges the alcohol industry to monitor its own efforts to avoid any depictions of dangerous or illegal use of alcohol, including appeals to anyone under the age of 21. Any beverage promotions that encourage excessive consumption, such as "happy hours," should be ended. Programs that encourage responsibility such as the *Designated Driver* should be encouraged.

Victim Issues

MADD is the largest anti-drunk driving victim assistance organization in the country. Because victims are frequently overburdened — financially and emotionally — as the result of alcohol- and other drug-impaired crashes, MADD has adopted the following public policy objectives.

Amendments for Victim Rights: Statutory Bills of Rights are only sporadically enforced but State Constitutional Amendments for Victim Rights would offer victims the right to be informed of, present at, and heard during the criminal justice process.

Bankruptcy Protection for Victims: Persons who kill or injure others as a result of alcohol- or other drug-impaired driving should not have the right to file bankruptcy in order to avoid paying restitution or civil judgments to their victims.

Compensation for Victims: Alcohol- and other drug-impaired crash victims should not be excluded from any State Crime Victim Compensation Program.

Dram Shop Recovery: Victims should have the right to seek financial recovery from establishments that irresponsibly provide alcohol to anyone under the age of 21 or serve alcohol to anyone past the point of intoxication.

Endangerment of Children Sanctions: Enhanced sanctions against convicted drunk drivers should be enforced when the offender was driving with a child in the vehicle.

MADD VICTIM SERVICES

Each of the 22,415 fatalities and 345,000 injuries incurred yearly is a unique and irreplaceable individual with a name, a family, and dreams that must now go unfulfilled. Each represents far more than a faceless number to his or her family and friends, who are now caught in the tragic ripple effect set off by each crash.

Crisis Intervention: Alcohol- and other drug-related crashes create a critical period in the lives of victims. MADD victim advocates provide emotional support to help victims cope with their grief and anger. In addition, victims receive printed materials to help them understand the grieving process and guide them through the criminal justice system.

Victim Support: MADD brings victims together in victim support groups to discuss their feelings and futures. Victims offer each other unique understanding and reassurance.

Victim Advocacy: Victims are offered a thorough explanation of the judicial process. MADD advocates clarify victim rights, accompany victims to court when necessary and follow up on the sentencing of offenders. MADD offers 40-hour beginning and annual Advanced Institutes to train victim advocates. MADD offers the *Victim Information Pamphlet* to inform victims about their rights in court proceedings and *Financial Recovery After A Drunk Driving Crash* to inform them about victim compensation, insurance and civil suits. The *MADDVOCATE* magazine provides up-to-date information for victims and victim advocates.

Victim Impact Panels: Judges or probation officers order convicted drunk drivers to attend a Victim Impact Panel as a component of their sentencing. The panel is composed of three or four victims of drunk driving crashes who tell their stories simply and from the heart. The goal of the program is to enable the offenders to understand their crime from the victim's perspective and choose to never again drink and drive.

Information and Referral: MADD chapters refer victims to other agencies that offer financial and legal information, as well as professional counseling, as requested.

6

Grassroots activism is the force behind MADD. Your unyielding determination, commitment, energy, courage and creativity, reduces the number of deaths and injuries from alcohol- and other drug-related driving.

You are helping us create a less violent future. Together we are making a difference because *WE ARE IN IT FOR LIVES.*

- Be responsible for your own thinking and actions about drunk driving — *DON'T DRINK AND DRIVE.*

- Encourage your family and friends to be responsible for their thinking and actions about drunk driving — *FRIENDS DON'T LET FRIENDS DRIVE DRUNK.*

- Be informed about the issue of drunk driving. Make yourself knowledgeable so that you can create conversations with others to raise their consciousness and support them in being responsible. MADD provides numerous written materials to educate you. We are just a telephone call away.

- Be actively involved at whatever level you can. If your community has a MADD chapter, volunteer your talent and time. Explore the possibility of organizing a chapter in your community, if a local chapter does not exist. Work with other resources in your community to fight alcohol- and other drug-related driving or create resources that are missing.

Thank you! You have expressed a commitment to end alcohol- and other drug related driving. For more information on MADD in your local community or how to get more involved, contact:

MADD National Office
511 E. John Carpenter Freeway, Suite 700
Irving, Texas 75062
214-744-MADD

Cookies

FOOD WRITERS' FAVORITES

EDITED BY BARBARA GIBBS OSTMANN AND JANE BAKER

Contents

Contributing Writers

Pamela Anderson, *Restaurant Business,* New York, NY
Barbara Mihalevich Arciero, *The Times,* Shreveport, LA
Rita Barrett, International Cookbook Services, White Plains, NY
Laura J. Barton, Free-lance Writer, Portland, OR
Betty Bernard, *Lake Charles American Press,* Lake Charles, LA
Barbara Bloch, International Cookbook Services, White Plains, NY
Beverly Bundy, *Fort Worth Star-Telegram,* Fort Worth, TX
Barbara Burklo, (Retired) *Santa Cruz Sentinel,* Santa Cruz, CA
Toni Burks, *Roanoke Times & World-News,* Roanoke, VA
Anne Byrn, *Atlanta Journal-Constitution,* Atlanta, GA
Narcisse S. Cadgène, Free-lance Writer, New York, NY
Evelyn Cairns, *The News-Herald Newspapers,* Southgate, MI
Sally Cappon, *Santa Barbara News-Press,* Santa Barbara, CA
Leona Carlson, (Retired) *Rockford Register Star,* Rockford, IL
Julie Cohen, Free-lance Writer, Toronto, Ontario, Canada
Carole Currie, *Asheville Citizen,* Asheville, NC
Louise F. Dodd, *Courier Herald,* Dublin, GA
Alma Drill, Universal Press Syndicate, Bethesda, MD
Beth Whitley Duke, *Amarillo Globe-News,* Amarillo, TX
Clara Eschmann, *Macon Telegraph and News,* Macon, GA
Carolyn Flournoy, *The Times,* Shreveport, LA
Paula M. Galusha, *Oklahoma Home & Lifestyle Magazine,* Tulsa, OK
Marie D. Galyean, *Idaho Press-Tribune,* Nampa, ID
June Ann Gladfelter, *The Express,* Easton, PA
Jane Witty Gould, *The Courier-News,* Bridgewater, NJ
Patricia G. Gray, *The Express,* Easton, PA
Paul Grondahl, *Albany Times Union,* Albany, NY
Lorrie Guttman, *Tallahassee Democrat,* Tallahassee, FL
Suzanne Hall, *The Chattanooga Times,* Chattanooga, TN

Constance Hay, Free-lance Food Writer, Washington, D.C.
Jim Hillibish, *The Repository*, Canton, OH
Stacy Lam, *Macon Telegraph and News*, Macon, GA
Lori Longbotham, *New York Post*, New York, NY
Joyce van Meer, Free-lance Writer, Washington, D.C.
Beth Winsten Orenstein, *The Express*, Easton, PA
Lou Seibert Pappas, *Times Tribune*, Palo Alto, CA
Frances Price, Food Columnist, Baltimore, MD
Joanna Pruess, Free-lance Writer, Montclair, NJ
Leni Reed, Food Columnist, Reston, VA
Doris Reynolds, *Naples Daily News*, Naples, FL
Jean Rogers, *Prevention Magazine*, Emmaus, PA
Norma Schonwetter, Syndicated Food Columnist, Oak Park, MI
Mary Denise Scourtes, *The Tampa Tribune*, Tampa, FL
Marlene Sorosky, Free-lance Food Writer, Hunt Valley, MD
Kathleen Stang, Free-lance Food Writer, Seattle, WA
Muriel Stevens, *Las Vegas Sun*, Las Vegas, NV
Jeanne Voltz, Cookbook Author, Pittsboro, NC
Ann Corell Wells, *The Grand Rapids Press*, Grand Rapids, MI

Introduction

Cookies, cookies and more cookies! When food editors and writers across the country were requested to contribute cookie recipes for this cookbook, the response was overwhelming. More than 500 recipes flooded into the publisher's office in a short period of time. It appears that everyone likes to prepare cookies. They have become all-American favorites.

The recipes in this cookbook include both the tried-and-true personal favorites of food writers and many regional specialties. There are a few "gourmet treats" that have several steps, but most of the recipes are quick to prepare and use ingredients that are stocked in most kitchens.

Cookie categories are difficult to define, but for this book the recipes have been divided into six categories: bar, drop, rolled (including those made with a rolling pin, cookie cutter or other special equipment, like pastry bags, cookie presses and cookie irons), molded (including balls, twists, crescents and other hand-made shapes), cookies that require no baking, and cookies that travel well. Bar cookies and drop cookies were the most popular contributions, but other categories show the diversity of cookie recipes.

From the hundreds of recipes submitted for the cookbook, few recipes were exactly the same. Obviously many cooks get creative with cookies, changing ingredients and cooking methods to suit individual tastes.

Each of the recipes in this cookbook also includes a brief introduction that tells you something about the recipe, which makes for enjoyable reading even when you are not in the mood to bake a batch of cookies.

We would like to make it clear that these recipes are the contributors' favorites. The publisher makes no claim that the recipes are original. When possible, credit has been given where credit is due. In many cases, however, the recipes have been handed down through families, with a variety of additions and subtractions. It is difficult, if not impossible, to say from whence they came. However, there is no doubt that each recipe is a tasty creation guaranteed to please family and friends.

Cookie Basics

Everyone likes to bake cookies — youngsters and adults, novices in the kitchen and experienced bakers. The recipes generally tell you all you need to know to prepare them. However, these tips might add to a cookie baker's expertise.

• Read the recipe all the way through before you begin. Make sure you have all the necessary ingredients and equipment on hand. Do not change or substitute ingredients until you have tried the recipe at least once. Varying the ingredients or cooking method can change results considerably.

• Use the appropriate liquid or dry measuring cups and be accurate in your measures. An extra set of measuring cups and spoons can save valuable time, especially when preparing several cookie recipes at one time.

• It is easier to prepare almost any recipe with a clear, clean counter space. This is especially true when preparing cookies.

• Fresh leavening, herbs and spices make a difference in the taste and texture of your cookies. Check the "use by" date on the label or container. If your supply is more than one year old, buy new baking powder, baking soda, spices and herbs.

• Making cookies the same size and shape will promote even baking and browning.

• When flour is added to the creamed mixture, mix just until all the ingredients are well blended. Overmixing makes the dough tough.

• Oven temperature is one of the most important factors in cookie baking. Follow recipe instructions carefully. Most cookie recipes require a preheated oven, so set the oven temperature 10 to 15 minutes before you are ready to begin baking. Use an oven thermometer for accurate temperatures.

• Bake one sheet of cookies at a time. Place the sheet on the center rack of the oven.

• Use a minute timer for accuracy. To prevent overbaking, check cookies two to five minutes before the minimum baking time.

• Overbaking dries out cookies. If that's a problem with one of your recipes, try baking the next batch one or two minutes less.

- Let baking pans cool between baking batches; re-grease pans, if necessary, between batches. Hot baking sheets will cause the dough to begin to melt, creating changes in the cookies' texture and shape.

- As a general rule, remove cookies from the baking pans quickly to prevent continued baking. However, refer to the recipe for specific instructions. Fragile or delicate cookies often are cooled on baking sheets a few minutes before being removed to wire racks to cool completely. This procedure helps to minimize breakage. Bar cookies should be left in the pan to cool, unless otherwise instructed in the recipe.

- Store crisp cookies in containers with loose-fitting lids. This will help keep them crisp.

- Store soft cookies in airtight containers. To help soft cookies retain their softness, place a small slice of apple in the container with the cookies.

- For best results when shipping cookies to friends or relatives: choose cookies that are sturdy, such as the ones in the "Cookies That Travel Well" section of this book. Put each type of cookie in separate rigid containers; mixing types of cookies in the same container can cause flavors and textures to change. Then use a large box filled with high-quality packing material to cushion the containers. Label each container, so the recipients do not have to rattle the containers and thereby break cookies.

- If you plan to freeze some of your cookie treasures, make sure you have enough freezer space before you begin. If necessary, reorganize the freezer to make room for the cookie containers.

Drop Cookies

Butter Pecan Crisps

Constance Hay
Free-lance Food Writer, Washington, D. C.

A fellow teacher shared this recipe with me when we both taught the same cooking class. It is one I treasure because the cookies are easy to prepare and have an excellent flavor. As their name implies, Butter Pecan Crisps have a light buttery taste with a special texture. Pecans add a special garnish. The cookies are elegant enough to serve at tea time or for dessert at a dinner party, accompanied by homemade ice cream or sorbet.

Makes 4 dozen cookies

1/2 cup unsalted butter, softened
1 cup granulated sugar
1 egg
1-1/2 cups buttermilk
   baking mix

1 teaspoon vanilla
48 pecan halves

In a large mixing bowl with an electric mixer or by hand, beat butter and sugar until fluffy. Add egg, buttermilk baking mix and vanilla. Mix thoroughly.

Drop dough by teaspoonfuls, about 3 inches apart, onto greased baking sheets. (The cookies spread out so be sure to leave space between them.) Put a pecan half in the center of each cookie and press down well.

Bake in a preheated 375-degree oven 8 or 9 minutes, or until done. Cookies must be watched carefully near the end of baking time. The baking sheet might need to be rotated for even browning. Immediately transfer cookies from baking sheets to wire racks to cool.

Carrot Cookies

Lorrie Guttman
Food Editor, *Tallahassee Democrat*, Tallahassee, Florida

When our paper held a recipe contest featuring carrots, we received an almost-overwhelming 110 entries. I managed to personally test some 45 of them, and these cookies came out on top, based on how quickly our tasters gobbled them up. Being drop cookies, they're easy to make. Oats, raisins, nuts and, of course, carrots add nutrients. The woman who won the contest said she'd had the recipe about 25 years and couldn't remember where she got it, but she's glad she did.

Makes about 3 dozen cookies

1/2 cup butter or margarine
1 cup firmly packed
  brown sugar
1/2 cup granulated sugar
2 eggs, well beaten
2 cups sifted all-purpose flour
2 teaspoons baking powder
1/2 teaspoon baking soda
1/2 teaspoon salt

1 teaspoon ground cinnamon
1/2 teaspoon ground nutmeg
2 cups old-fashioned or
  quick-cooking rolled oats,
  uncooked
1 cup raisins
1 cup shredded (not too finely)
  carrots
1 cup chopped nuts

In a large mixing bowl with an electric mixer, beat butter, brown sugar and granulated sugar until well mixed. Add eggs; mix well. Sift together flour, baking powder, baking soda, salt, cinnamon and nutmeg; add to butter mixture and mix well. Stir in oats, raisins, carrots and nuts.

Drop dough by tablespoonfuls onto ungreased baking sheets. Flatten slightly. Bake in a preheated 350-degree oven 25 to 30 minutes, or until done. Transfer to racks to cool.

Chocolate-Date-Nut Kisses

Jane Witty Gould
Free-lance Food Writer, Bridgewater, New Jersey

If there is one gastronomic gap at the Seder table, it is the lack of imaginative desserts. According to Passover dietary laws, any form of "hametz" (flour or leavening) is strictly forbidden, because when the Jews escaped from Egypt there was no time to allow the bread to rise. As a reminder of the Jews' historic exodus, the only natural leavening allowed during Passover is eggs, which is one reason why sponge cakes are so popular at this time of year. The egg is also used for meringue, a lovely light dessert base as well as a pie topping. Meringue also makes excellent crunchy drop clusters. When chocolate morsels and chopped dates are added, the cookies are not only strictly kosher but also strictly delicious.

Makes 2 dozen cookies

2 egg whites
1 cup confectioners' sugar
2/3 cup pitted, coarsely chopped dates
1 cup coarsely chopped walnuts
1 cup semisweet chocolate morsels

In a medium mixing bowl with an electric mixer, beat egg whites until stiff and glossy. Add confectioners' sugar, 1 tablespoon at a time, beating until stiff after each addition. Fold in dates, walnuts and chocolate morsels.

Drop mixture by rounded teaspoonfuls onto two baking sheets lined with ungreased parchment paper, putting 1 dozen cookies on each sheet.

Bake on first and third racks of a preheated 300-degree oven for 15 minutes. Exchange positions of pans on racks. Reduce oven temperature to 275 degrees. Bake for 15 minutes. Turn off oven. Leave cookies in oven, undisturbed, for 2 hours.

Store cooled cookies in airtight containers.

Choco-Nut Happy Drops

Marie D. Galyean
Lifestyle and Food Editor, *Idaho Press-Tribune*, Nampa, Idaho

As a young mother with two children, I married a man with custody of his six children. This gave me the challenge of quite a blend of tastes to cater to when preparing meals.

Desserts were a special problem, and I frantically combined every recipe I could think of to come up with family pleasers. These delightfully chocolatey, soft cookies with a delicate touch of peanut butter won the popularity poll, and remain favorites even though all the kids are grown and gone. When they return for visits, Happy Drops are one of the first requests.

Let your kids help by scooping out the dough with a melon baller.

Makes about 4 dozen cookies

1/2 cup butter or margarine, softened	1-1/3 cups all-purpose flour
1 cup firmly packed brown sugar	1/2 cup unsweetened cocoa powder
1 egg, beaten	1-1/2 teaspoons baking powder
1 teaspoon vanilla	1/4 teaspoon salt
1/2 cup evaporated milk	1 cup peanut butter morsels
	1/3 cup finely chopped pecans

In a large mixing bowl with an electric mixer, blend butter and brown sugar, then beat on medium speed about 2 minutes. Add egg, vanilla and evaporated milk. Beat until smooth. Combine flour, cocoa, baking powder and salt in a separate bowl. With mixer on low speed, gradually add flour mixture to butter mixture, mixing until blended. Stir in peanut butter morsels and pecans.

Cover dough and refrigerate it for about 1 hour. Using the large end of a melon baller or a teaspoon, drop rounded spoonfuls of chilled dough onto greased baking sheets, leaving at least an inch between drops.

Bake in a preheated 350-degree oven 12 to 15 minutes, or until set. Let cool on baking sheets for 1 minute, then transfer to wire racks to cool completely.

Coconut Chocolate Chippers

Toni Burks

Food Editor, *Roanoke Times & World-News,* Roanoke, Virginia

Chocolate and orange are delicious partners, and they're showcased nicely in this macaroon-like confection. These cookies are crisp, not soft, and a bit chewy. Don't worry about them baking into irregular shapes. A few lopsided cookies are a good indication that they're homemade!

Makes 3 to 3-1/2 dozen cookies

2 eggs
3/4 cup granulated sugar
1/2 cup all-purpose flour
1 tablespoon butter, melted
   and cooled
2 cups shredded coconut

1 package (6 ounces)
   semisweet chocolate morsels
1-1/2 teaspoons grated
   orange peel
1 teaspoon vanilla

In a large mixing bowl with an electric mixer on low speed, beat eggs until foamy. Gradually add sugar; continue beating until mixture is quite thick and lemon colored. Fold in flour and butter. Stir in coconut, chocolate morsels, orange peel and vanilla.

Drop mixture by teaspoonfuls onto greased and lightly floured baking sheets. Bake in a preheated 325-degree oven 10 to 15 minutes, or until firm to the touch and lightly golden.

Let cool slightly on baking sheets, then use a spatula to transfer cookies to wire rack to cool completely.

Note: These cookies freeze well.

Chocolate Meringues

Barbara Burklo

Food Editor (Retired), *Santa Cruz Sentinel,* Santa Cruz, California

When our family was living in the pretty little village of Columbiana, Ohio, a neighbor, Joan Jones, shared this cookie recipe with me. These airy little cookies contain rich tastes of chocolate and nuts. Coconut can be added, if desired.

Makes 2 to 3 dozen cookies

2 egg whites
1/8 teaspoon salt
1/8 teaspoon cream of tartar
1 teaspoon vanilla
3/4 cup granulated sugar

1 package (6 ounces) semisweet chocolate morsels
1/4 cup chopped walnuts
1 can (3-1/2 ounces) shredded coconut (optional)

In a large mixing bowl with an electric mixer on medium speed, beat egg whites, salt, cream of tartar and vanilla until soft peaks form. Gradually add sugar, beating until stiff peaks form. Carefully fold in chocolate morsels, walnuts and coconut.

Place plain paper (such as white typing paper) on baking sheets. Drop mixture by rounded teaspoonfuls onto paper, leaving space between cookies to allow for spreading.

Bake in a preheated 300-degree oven 25 minutes, or until cookies are very delicately golden. Let cool slightly before removing from paper.

Cranberry Cookies

Lorrie Guttman

Food Editor, *Tallahassee Democrat,* Tallahassee, Florida

I'm always happy to see fresh cranberries arrive at the produce counters in the fall, and I buy many bags to use for cranberry sauce. But I also like to bake with cranberries, so I stock up for recipes such as this one. You can take cranberries straight from the freezer, rinse them, and then toss them into a blender or food processor for coarse chopping. These cookies are flavored with some of Florida's favorite beverage — orange juice. For the nuts, I use pecans because we have a pecan tree in our front yard.

Makes about 11 dozen small cookies

1/2 cup margarine, softened	1/2 teaspoon salt
1 cup granulated sugar	1 teaspoon baking powder
3/4 cup firmly packed brown sugar	1/4 teaspoon baking soda
1/4 cup milk	2-1/2 cups coarsely chopped cranberries
2 tablespoons orange juice	1 cup chopped pecans or other nuts
1 egg	
3 cups all-purpose flour	

In a large mixing bowl with an electric mixer, beat margarine, granulated sugar and brown sugar until mixed. Stir in milk, orange juice and egg. Mix in flour, salt, baking powder, baking soda, cranberries and nuts.

Drop dough by teaspoonfuls, about 2 inches apart, onto greased baking sheets. Bake in a preheated 375-degree oven 10 to 15 minutes, or until done. Transfer to racks to cool.

Double Chocolate Cookies

Suzanne Hall

Food Editor, *The Chattanooga Times,* Chattanooga, Tennessee

Mrs. Miriam Axley may be in her 80s, but at least once a week she still cooks supper for her "family." And what a family it is. For nearly 20 years, this younger-than-her-years cook has been preparing Wednesday night supper for members of Chattanooga's Second Presbyterian Church. She tries to keep her menus well balanced and nutritious, but she also knows that kids love cookies — such as these.

Makes about 4 dozen cookies

2 cups all-purpose flour, sifted
1 teaspoon baking soda
1/4 cup granulated sugar
1 package (4 ounces) instant chocolate pudding mix
1 cup butter or margarine
3/4 cup firmly packed light brown sugar

1 teaspoon vanilla
2 eggs
1 package (12 ounces) semisweet chocolate morsels
1 cup chopped nuts (optional)

Sift together flour, baking soda, sugar and dry pudding mix.

In a large mixing bowl with an electric mixer, beat butter, brown sugar, vanilla and eggs until light and fluffy. Gradually beat in flour mixture. Stir in chocolate morsels and nuts.

Drop dough by heaping teaspoonfuls onto lightly greased baking sheets. Bake in a preheated 375-degree oven about 10 minutes, or until done. Transfer to racks to cool.

Dried Fruit Oatmeal Cookies

Lori Longbotham
Food Columnist, *New York Post*, New York, New York

These guilt-free cookies are high in fiber and low in fat, and they are delicious. These would be great cookies for after-school snacks—they're old-fashioned oatmeal raisin cookies with a couple of new twists.

You might substitute other dried fruits for the ones listed—dried peaches or prunes would be wonderful. You might also substitute margarine for the butter or egg substitute for the egg.

Makes 3 dozen cookies

1-1/4 cups old-fashioned
   rolled oats, uncooked
1/2 cup all-purpose flour
1/2 cup wheat germ
1/2 cup sesame seeds
1/4 cup oat bran
1/4 cup golden raisins
1/4 cup minced dried apricots
1/4 cup finely chopped
   dried figs
1 teaspoon baking powder

1/2 teaspoon salt
1/2 cup unsalted butter
1/2 cup firmly packed dark
   brown sugar
1/4 cup granulated sugar
1 egg
1 teaspoon vanilla
1 teaspoon grated lemon zest
1 to 2 tablespoons water
   (optional)

In a medium bowl, combine oats, flour, wheat germ, sesame seeds, oat bran, raisins, apricots, figs, baking powder and salt. Stir until well mixed.

In a large mixing bowl with an electric mixer, beat butter, brown sugar and granulated sugar until well mixed. Add egg; blend. Add vanilla and lemon zest; mix well. Add oats mixture; mix well. If dough is dry, add 1 to 2 tablespoons water.

Drop dough by tablespoonfuls onto non-stick baking sheets and flatten slightly. Bake in a preheated 375-degree oven 10 to 12 minutes, or until golden and edges are slightly brown. Let cool 3 minutes on baking sheets, then use with a metal spatula to transfer cookies to wire racks to cool completely.

Farm Cookies

Lorrie Guttman

Food Editor, *Tallahassee Democrat*, Tallahassee, Florida

If, like me, you end up with small amounts of dry cereal left over from various boxes, you'll be glad to have this recipe. It calls for corn flakes, but almost any other dry cereal could be substituted. I don't substitute for the Grape Nuts because that cereal is a favorite with my family, and we like its taste in recipes.

Makes about 6 dozen cookies

1 cup solid vegetable shortening
1-1/2 cups firmly packed
  brown sugar
1/3 cup honey
2 eggs
2 teaspoons almond extract
1/3 cup lemon-flavor yogurt
3-1/2 cups unsifted all-purpose
  flour
1 teaspoon baking soda
1 teaspoon salt
3 cups corn flakes
1/2 cup chopped peanuts
1/4 cup wheat germ
1 cup Grape Nuts cereal
1/2 cup shredded coconut

In a large mixing bowl with an electric mixer, beat shortening, brown sugar, honey and eggs until creamy. Add almond extract and yogurt. Mix well. Add flour, baking soda and salt; mix until well combined. Add corn flakes, peanuts, wheat germ, cereal and coconut; stir by hand until blended.

Drop dough by rounded teaspoonfuls onto ungreased baking sheets. Flatten cookies with fork or fingers. Bake in a preheated 375-degree oven 8 to 10 minutes, or until light golden brown.

Store these crunchy cookies in an airtight container.

Variations: You can reduce the amount of almond extract, substitute coconut extract, or totally omit the extract. You can use plain yogurt or any other light-colored yogurt, such as peach or strawberry. (Darker colors give the cookies an unappetizing color.) You can use almost any kind of dry cereal you would like as a substitute for part or all of the corn flakes and Grape Nuts. You can use other nuts instead of peanuts. Chopped fresh or dried fruit can be added in any amount you like.

Irish Oatmeal Hermits

Joanna Pruess

Free-lance Writer, Montclair, New Jersey

These cookies could be called "true grit," because of the crunchy toasted oats, chewy coconut and dried fruits they contain. The toasted Irish oats, found in cans, lend a healthful nuttiness to these Hermits, and the mixed fruit bits are a fast and helpful addition.

Makes 2 dozen cookies

1 cup Irish rolled oats (not the quick-cooking kind), uncooked

3/4 cup unsalted butter, at room temperature

1/2 cup firmly packed light brown sugar

2 eggs

1 teaspoon orange extract

3/4 cup shredded coconut (sweetened or unsweetened)

1 cup unbleached or all-purpose flour

1 teaspoon salt

1 teaspoon baking powder

1 teaspoon baking soda

1-1/2 teaspoons ground cinnamon

1-1/2 teaspoons ground coriander

1-1/2 cups chopped mixed dried fruit

Spread a thin layer of oats on a baking sheet; toast in a preheated 325-degree oven about 15 minutes, or until lightly browned. Set aside to cool.

In a medium mixing bowl with an electric mixer or wooden spoon, beat butter until light and fluffy. Stir in brown sugar, then the eggs, orange extract and coconut.

Sift flour, salt, baking powder, baking soda, cinnamon and coriander over butter mixture; mix well. Add toasted oats and dried fruit; stir to blend.

Lightly grease baking sheets or line with parchment paper. Drop dough by rounded tablespoonfuls onto prepared pans, leaving about 3 inches between cookies. Bake in the middle of a preheated 325-degree oven 12 to 14 minutes, or until lightly colored around the outside and puffed in the middle. Do not overbake.

Let cookies cool on baking sheets for 5 minutes before transferring them to wire racks to cool completely.

Store in airtight tins. They will keep at least one week.

Kitchen Sink Cookies

Paul Grondahl

Feature Writer, *Albany Times Union*, Albany, New York

My wife's chocolate chip cookies are famous at the newspaper, where they are forever getting passed around to appreciative reporters and editors in the cafeteria at lunchtime. The paper's food critic gives them four stars.

Because I don't like store-bought cookies, Hope makes a few dozen of her specials for my lunch each week. I never tire of Hope's chocolate chip cookies, but she grows weary of baking the same thing over and over, so she started experimenting with the recipe and tossed in whatever ingredients were around — hence the name "kitchen sink." Hope sometimes includes walnuts and other nuts, but this version seems to be the reporters' (tough critics, all) favorite.

Makes 3 to 4 dozen cookies

1 cup unsalted butter or margarine
3/4 cup firmly packed light brown sugar
1 teaspoon vanilla
2 eggs
2-1/4 cups all-purpose flour
2 cups quick-cooking or old-fashioned rolled oats, uncooked

1 teaspoon baking soda
1 teaspoon ground cinnamon
1/4 teaspoon ground nutmeg
1 cup raisins
2 cups semisweet chocolate morsels

In a large mixing bowl with an electric mixer, beat butter and brown sugar until light and smooth. Add vanilla; beat well. Add eggs, one at a time, beating well after each addition.

In another mixing bowl, combine flour, oats, baking soda, cinnamon and nutmeg. Add flour mixture to butter mixture; blend well. Fold in raisins and chocolate morsels. Mix thoroughly.

Drop dough by rounded teaspoonfuls onto ungreased baking sheets. Bake in a preheated 375-degree oven 8 to 10 minutes, or until lightly browned. Transfer to racks to cool.

Lemon Meringue Cookies

Lori Longbotham
Food Columnist, *New York Post*, New York City, New York

*Everyone loves lemon meringue pie — and they also
will love these lighter-than-air, meltingly sweet, lemon
cookies. The cookies have the same terrific lemon meringue pie flavor, but they last much longer and are
much more portable. They're a cinch to make, taking
only about 15 minutes to toss together. Enjoy them even
more knowing that they have only about 20 calories per
cookie and are very low in fat.*

Makes about 2 dozen cookies

3 egg whites, at room
  temperature
1/4 teaspoon cream of tartar

6 tablespoons granulated sugar
1 tablespoon grated lemon zest

In large mixing bowl with electric mixer, beat egg whites until
foamy. Add cream of tartar; beat on high speed until soft peaks form.
Beat in sugar, 1 tablespoon at a time; continue beating until stiff and
shiny peaks form. Gently fold lemon zest into beaten egg whites.

Drop mixture by heaping tablespoonfuls onto two buttered and
floured baking sheets. Bake in a preheated 250-degree oven 1 hour.
Turn off oven; do not open oven door. Leave the cookies, undisturbed,
in the oven for 1 hour. Then transfer to wire racks to cool completely.
Store in a tightly covered container.

Luscious Lemon Drops

Carolyn Flournoy
Cooking Columnist, *The Times*, Shreveport, Louisiana

This is one of those recipes using a packaged mix that "went around" several years ago. I experimented with several variations of my own and came up with a cookie that my family and friends say is a real winner. Ardent lemon lovers will be enchanted — and ask for more, more, more.

Makes about 4 dozen cookies

1 package (18-1/4 ounces) lemon-flavor cake mix
1 container (4-1/2 ounces) frozen non-dairy whipped topping, thawed

1 egg, beaten
1-1/2 teaspoons lemon juice
1 teaspoon grated lemon peel
1/2 cup confectioners' sugar, sifted

In a large mixing bowl, combine dry cake mix, whipped topping, egg, lemon juice and lemon peel; stir to mix well, but do not overmix.

Drop dough by teaspoonfuls into confectioners' sugar, turning to coat well. Place balls, 1-1/2 inches apart, on well-greased baking sheets. Bake in a preheated 350-degree oven 12 minutes, or until done. Remove from baking sheets immediately and let cool on wire racks.

Macadamia Nut and White Chocolate Cookies

Beverly Bundy
Food Editor, *Fort Worth Star-Telegram*, Fort Worth, Texas

*These wonderfully rich — and expensive to make —
cookies are too good for the kitchen cookie jar. Serve
them after a meal for a rich, yet homespun, dessert.*

Makes 2 dozen cookies

2 cups all-purpose flour
1 teaspoon baking soda
1/2 teaspoon salt
3/4 cup unsalted butter, softened
1 cup firmly packed light
  brown sugar
3/4 cup granulated sugar

2 eggs, at room temperature
1 teaspoon vanilla
12 ounces white chocolate,
  cut into 1/4-inch chunks
1-1/2 cups coarsely chopped
  macadamia nuts

Cover two baking sheets with parchment paper or aluminum foil; set aside.

Sift flour, baking soda and salt into a medium bowl; set aside.

In a large mixing bowl with an electric mixer on low speed, beat butter for 30 to 45 seconds, or until butter is creamy. Gradually add brown sugar and granulated sugar; beat on medium speed for 1 to 2 minutes, or until mixture is light and fluffy. Add eggs, one at a time, beating well between each addition. Add vanilla. Using a wooden spoon, stir in reserved flour mixture. Add white chocolate chunks and nuts; stir until well combined.

Use a 1/4-cup measuring cup to form cookies; pack dough into measuring cup so it is even with edge. Drop dough onto prepared baking sheets, leaving about 3 inches between cookies. Flatten dough slightly with palm of hand.

Bake on center rack of a preheated 300-degree oven 20 to 25 minutes, or until lightly browned around the edges but still slightly soft in center. Let cookies cool on baking sheets for 3 to 5 minutes, then transfer cookies to wire racks to cool completely.

Oatmeal Applesauce Cookies

Stacy Lam

Reporter, *Macon Telegraph and News,* Macon, Georgia

This variation on the oatmeal cookie is neither chewy nor crunchy, but moist — more like cake. Whenever I take cookies to a party or to a friend, these are the cookies I take. Oatmeal cookies are an old favorite, but this version is new to most people.

The cookies should be stored in a container by themselves. Other cookies could draw the moisture from these cookies, leaving them dry and crumbly. Half an apple placed in the container will help keep the cookies moist.

Makes about 3-1/2 dozen cookies

1/2 cup solid vegetable shortening
1 cup granulated sugar
1 egg
1-3/4 cups sifted all-purpose flour
1/2 teaspoon baking soda
1/2 teaspoon baking powder
1/2 teaspoon salt
1 teaspoon ground cinnamon
1/2 teaspoon ground cloves
1/2 teaspoon ground nutmeg
1/2 cup raisins
1 cup quick-cooking or old-fashioned rolled oats, uncooked
1 cup applesauce

In a large mixing bowl with an electric mixer, beat shortening and sugar until soft, smooth and creamy. Stir in egg.

Sift flour, baking soda, baking powder, salt, cinnamon, cloves and nutmeg into a separate bowl. Stir in raisins and oats.

Add flour mixture to shortening mixture in three portions alternating with applesauce in two portions. Beat the mixture by hand until well blended.

Drop dough by tablespoonfuls onto greased baking sheets. Bake in a preheated 375-degree oven 15 minutes, or until done. Let cookies cool on baking sheets a few minutes before transferring them to racks to cool completely.

Oatmeal Cookies

Clara Eschmann
Food Columnist, *Macon Telegraph and News,* Macon, Georgia

This recipe came originally on the side of an oatmeal box. But I made some changes to suit my family's tastes. Judging from the splatters on the recipe card, I can tell it was used often. I still make these for my grandsons because I think the ingredients are healthful and the cookies delicious.

Makes 6 to 8 dozen cookies, depending on size

3/4 cup solid vegetable shortening
1 cup firmly packed brown sugar
1/2 cup granulated sugar
1 egg
1/4 cup water
1 cup all-purpose flour
1 teaspoon salt

1/2 teaspoon baking soda
1 teaspoon vanilla
1 teaspoon ground cinnamon
1/2 teaspoon ground allspice
3-1/2 cups quick-cooking rolled oats, uncooked
1/2 cup finely chopped pecans or other nuts
1 cup raisins

In a large mixing bowl with an electric mixer, beat shortening, brown sugar, granulated sugar and egg until mixed. Mix in water.

In another bowl, combine flour, salt and baking soda; add to shortening mixture and mix well. Stir in vanilla, cinnamon and allspice. Fold in oats, pecans and raisins, mixing well. (This last step should be done by hand to make sure all ingredients are thoroughly blended.)

Drop dough by teaspoonfuls onto greased baking sheets. Bake in preheated 350-degree oven 12 to 15 minutes, or until done. Transfer to racks to cool.

Oatmeal Gems

Toni Burks

Food Editor, *Roanoke Times & World-News*, Roanoke, Virginia

Here's an oatmeal cookie for those who occasionally enjoy a soft version of the classic cookie. These bake up plump and mellow, heady with spices and crunchy with nuts and oats. I baked these cookies for my children's lunch boxes. And I continue to bake them now, even though my family is grown, so I have treats when other children come to call.

Makes 6 to 7 dozen cookies

1 cup raisins
1 cup water
3/4 cup solid vegetable shortening
1-1/2 cups granulated sugar
2 eggs
1 teaspoon vanilla
2-1/2 cups sifted all-purpose flour

1/2 teaspoon baking powder
1 teaspoon baking soda
1 teaspoon salt (optional)
1 teaspoon ground cinnamon
1 teaspoon ground cloves
2 cups old-fashioned rolled oats, uncooked
1/2 cup chopped walnuts or pecans

Combine raisins and water in small saucepan. Simmer over low heat 20 to 30 minutes, or until raisins are nicely plumped. Drain liquid from raisins into measuring cup. If necessary, add enough additional water to raisin liquid to measure 1/2 cup. Set drained raisins and 1/2 cup raisin liquid aside to cool.

In a large mixing bowl with an electric mixer, beat shortening, sugar, eggs and vanilla until smooth and creamy. Stir in reserved 1/2 cup raisin liquid.

Sift the sifted flour, baking powder, baking soda, salt, cinnamon and cloves into another mixing bowl. Stir flour mixture into shortening mixture with a spoon. Stir in oats, nuts and reserved raisins; mix well.

Drop dough by rounded teaspoonfuls, about 2 inches apart, onto ungreased baking sheets. Bake in a preheated 375-degree oven 8 to 10 minutes, or until lightly browned.

Note: These cookies freeze well.

Persimmon Cookies

Sally Cappon

Food Writer, *Santa Barbara News-Press,* Santa Barbara, California

Persimmon trees give Santa Barbara much of its scarlet and orange autumn foliage in late October and November. With an abundance of the sweet Asian fruit, we look for ways to use the soft pulp. A favorite is this persimmon cookie, adapted from a recipe given to me by a long-time neighbor.

Makes 3 dozen cookies

1 cup persimmon pulp
1/2 teaspoon baking soda
1/2 cup butter or margarine
1 cup granulated sugar
1/2 teaspoon ground cinnamon
1/2 teaspoon ground cloves
1/2 teaspoon ground nutmeg
2 cups all-purpose flour
1 cup chopped walnuts
1 cup raisins
1 egg, beaten

In a mixing bowl, combine persimmon pulp and baking soda. Set aside.

In a separate bowl with an electric mixer on medium speed, beat butter and sugar until smooth and creamy. Combine cinnamon, cloves, nutmeg and flour; stir in walnuts and raisins. Add flour mixture to butter mixture; mix well.

Add egg to reserved persimmon mixture; mix. Add persimmon mixture to butter mixture; blend well.

Drop dough by teaspoonfuls onto greased baking sheets. Bake in a preheated 300-degree oven 25 to 30 minutes, or until done. Transfer to racks to cool.

Pistachio and Raisin Caramel Cookies

Lou Seibert Pappas

Food Editor, *Times Tribune,* Palo Alto, California

Steel-cut oats, available in specialty markets, lend a wonderful chewiness to this versatile cookie that can have many flavor variations. (If steel-cut oats are not available, either quick-cooking or old-fashioned rolled oats will do.)

The recipe started out decades ago as a favorite dark chocolate chip cookie, developed by a family that produced small batches of stone-ground flour at their Oregon farm. Over the years, it has taken on golden raisins, snipped dried apricots, white chocolate and pistachios, pecans, almonds and macadamia nuts.

Makes about 2-1/2 dozen cookies

1/2 cup margarine or butter
1/2 cup granulated sugar
1/4 cup firmly packed brown sugar
1/2 teaspoon vanilla
1 egg
1 cup stone-ground or all-purpose flour
3/4 cup steel-cut oats (or old-fashioned or quick-cooking oats), uncooked
1/2 teaspoon baking soda
1/4 teaspoon salt
1 cup golden or dark raisins or snipped dried apricots or 6 ounces white or semisweet chocolate morsels
1/2 cup coarsely chopped pistachios, almonds, walnuts, pecans or macadamia nuts

In a large mixing bowl with an electric mixer, beat margarine, granulated sugar and brown sugar until light and fluffy. Mix in vanilla and egg. Stir together flour, oats, baking soda and salt; add to butter mixture and mix until blended. Add raisins and nuts, mixing well.

Drop dough by teaspoonfuls onto greased baking sheets. Bake in a preheated 350-degree oven 8 to 10 minutes, or until golden brown. Transfer to racks to cool.

Note: These cookies freeze well.

Pumpkin Cookies

Jim Hillibish

Food Editor, *The Repository,* Canton, Ohio

For the frugal, these cookies fit. How many times have you assembled a pumpkin pie, only to find you've got a cup or two of cooked pumpkin left over? And what does one do with cooked pumpkin? Unless the dog's a vegetarian, you make cookies, of course.

These pumpkin cookies are excellent. Don't hesitate to dress them up with raisins and nuts. They are an old-fashioned batter cookie of simple means, undoubtedly a favorite on pumpkin-patch farms. Don't wait until Halloween to try them.

Makes about 3 dozen cookies

1/2 cup butter
1-1/4 cups granulated sugar
2 eggs, beaten
1-1/2 cups cooked or canned pumpkin
1/2 teaspoon salt
1/2 teaspoon ground cinnamon
1/2 teaspoon ground nutmeg
1/4 teaspoon ground ginger
1 teaspoon lemon extract
2-1/2 cups sifted all-purpose flour
4 teaspoons baking powder
1 cup raisins (optional)
1 cup chopped nuts (optional)

In a large mixing bowl with an electric mixer, beat butter and sugar until smooth and creamy. Add eggs, mixing well. In a separate bowl, blend pumpkin with salt, cinnamon, nutmeg and ginger. Fold pumpkin mixture into the butter mixture. Add lemon extract; mix well.

Sift together flour and baking powder; add to batter and mix until smooth. Add raisins and nuts; mix well.

Drop batter by teaspoonfuls onto greased baking sheets. Bake in a preheated 400-degree oven 13 to 15 minutes, checking for doneness after 13 minutes. Transfer to racks to cool.

Pummies

Joyce van Meer
Free-lance Writer, Washington, D.C.

Pumpkin is too good (and healthful) to use only at Thanksgiving in pie. Add it to pancakes or muffins, or try it in these cake-like cookies which stay soft and delicious. The cookies can be varied by using traditional pumpkin pie spice with raisins and nuts or by trying more adventurous combinations such as maple, lemon and ginger, or my special favorite, rum flavoring and chocolate.

Makes about 5 dozen cookies

1/2 cup margarine or butter,
   at room temperature
1/2 cup firmly packed
   brown sugar
1/2 cup granulated sugar
1 egg, lightly beaten
1 cup cooked or canned
   pumpkin
2 cups all-purpose flour
1 teaspoon baking soda
1/2 teaspoon salt

*ONE of the following
groups of ingredients*:
2 teaspoons rum flavoring
1 cup semisweet chocolate
   morsels
OR:
2 teaspoons maple flavoring
1 teaspoon grated lemon zest
1/2 cup chopped crystallized
   ginger
OR:
1 tablespoon pumpkin pie spice
1 cup raisins
1/4 cup coarsely chopped nuts

In a large mixing bowl with an electric mixer, beat margarine, brown sugar and granulated sugar. Stir in egg and pumpkin. Add rum flavoring or maple flavoring, if using.

Mix flour with baking soda and salt. Add lemon zest or pumpkin pie spice, if using. Add flour mixture to pumpkin mixture, stirring until well mixed. Stir in chocolate morsels, ginger, or raisins and nuts, if using.

Drop dough by teaspoonfuls onto lightly greased baking sheets. Bake in a preheated 375-degree oven 15 minutes, or until cookies are firm. Remove from baking sheets immediately and allow to cool completely before storing.

Rich and Chewy Chocolate-Orange Cookies

Pamela Anderson

Food Editor, *Restaurant Business,* New York, New York

Dress up these luxurious chocolate cookies by drizzling melted white chocolate over their tops after they have cooled. For more professional-looking results, use a pastry bag fitted with a 1/8-inch round tip to pipe the white chocolate onto the cookies.

Makes 4 dozen cookies

1-3/4 cups all-purpose flour
1/4 teaspoon baking soda
1/3 cup unsweetened cocoa
    powder
1 cup unsalted butter, softened
1 cup granulated sugar
1/2 cup firmly packed dark
    brown sugar

1 teaspoon vanilla
1 egg
1/2 tablespoon grated orange
    zest
3 tablespoons orange juice

In a medium bowl, combine flour, baking soda and cocoa; set aside.

In a large mixing bowl with an electric mixer on medium speed, beat butter until light and fluffy. Add granulated sugar and brown sugar; beat until smooth. Beat in vanilla and egg, then orange zest and orange juice. With mixer on low speed, gradually beat in reserved flour mixture.

Drop dough by teaspoonfuls, about 2 inches apart, onto baking sheets lined with parchment paper. Bake in a preheated 350-degree oven about 9 minutes, or until cookies are firm to the touch. Let cookies cool slightly on baking sheets, then use a spatula to transfer them to a wire rack to cool completely.

Note: Cookies can be stored in an airtight container up to one week.

Salted Peanut Cookies

Ann Corell Wells
Food Editor, *The Grand Rapids Press*, Grand Rapids, Michigan

These cookies always bring back fond childhood memories. When my brothers and I were youngsters spending our summers on Lake Michigan, there was a general store in our town — the old-fashioned kind of store with wooden barrels filled with pickles, crackers, flour, sugar, and yes, a pot-belly stove around which the men gathered.

Mrs. Beckman, who owned the store with her husband, always made these cookies, and, of course, there were plenty of samples for the little children coming into the store. We begged to go to the store just for Mrs. Beckman's salted peanut cookies. They were my favorite cookies in the '40s, and they still are today.

Makes 5 to 6 dozen cookies

1 cup margarine	1 teaspoon baking powder
2 cups firmly packed brown sugar	1 teaspoon baking soda
	1 cup Wheaties cereal
2 eggs, beaten	2 cups quick-cooking rolled
2 cups all-purpose flour	oats, uncooked
1/2 teaspoon salt	1 cup chopped salted peanuts

In a large mixing bowl with an electric mixer, beat margarine and brown sugar until fluffy. Blend in eggs. Sift together flour, salt, baking powder and baking soda. Add sifted flour mixture to margarine mixture; mix well. Stir in cereal and oats, then stir in peanuts.

Drop dough by teaspoonfuls onto lightly greased baking sheets. Press with a fork to flatten. Bake in a preheated 400-degree oven 10 to 12 minutes, or until done.

Note: These cookies have never lasted long enough at our house to freeze any, but I am sure they would freeze well.

Soft Ginger Creams with Glossy Orange Frosting

Betty Bernard

Food Editor, *Lake Charles American Press*, Lake Charles, Louisiana

Reba Beard, who is the city desk editor here at the American Press, *loves to bake. She makes the best breads and cookies; best of all, she shares them with all of us. This is one of her favorite cookie recipes.*

Makes 5 to 7 dozen cookies

2 cups sifted all-purpose flour
1/2 teaspoon baking soda
1/4 teaspoon salt
2 teaspoons ground ginger
1/4 teaspoon ground cinnamon
3/4 cup margarine

1 cup firmly packed light brown sugar
3 tablespoons light molasses
1 egg
1/2 cup dairy sour cream

Glossy Orange Frosting:

1 egg white, slightly beaten
1-1/2 cups confectioners' sugar
1 tablespoon margarine, melted

1/8 teaspoon salt
1/2 teaspoon vanilla
1/4 teaspoon orange extract

Sift together flour, baking soda, salt, ginger and cinnamon; set aside.

In a mixing bowl with an electric mixer, beat margarine until softened. Add brown sugar gradually, beating until fluffy. Blend in molasses. Add egg; beat thoroughly. Alternately add reserved flour mixture one-third at a time and sour cream one-half at a time, beating until blended after each addition.

Drop dough by teaspoonfuls, about 2 inches apart, onto lightly greased baking sheets. Bake in a preheated 375-degree oven 8 to 10 minutes, or until done. Transfer cookies to wire racks to cool.

For Glossy Orange Frosting: In a small bowl, combine egg white and confectioners' sugar. Add melted margarine, salt, vanilla and orange extract. Beat until smooth. If frosting is too thin, add a little more confectioners' sugar; if too thick, add a little more margarine. Use to frost Soft Ginger Creams.

Walnut-Cocoa Drops with Mocha Frosting

Jeanne Voltz
Cookbook Author, Pittsboro, North Carolina

Mrs. Wills, my first Girl Scout leader, wore violet perfume and taught us 12-year-olds how to bake cookies and put on a proper tea for our mothers. I remember this cookie from her repertoire better than the eggs cooked on hot rocks and other crude cuisine that we practiced when we went to Camp Juliette Lowe in the Southern Appalachians. I've taken this cookie to home-room parties in my children's schools and to bake sales. I've baked thousands of them for treats at home.

Makes about 5 dozen cookies

1 cup granulated sugar	2 teaspoons baking powder
1/2 cup unsweetened cocoa powder	1 teaspoon baking soda
2/3 cup vegetable oil	1/4 teaspoon salt
1 egg	1 cup buttermilk or plain yogurt
2-1/4 cups all-purpose or unbleached flour	1 teaspoon vanilla
	1/2 cup chopped walnuts

Mocha Frosting:

1 tablespoon butter or margarine, softened	3 tablespoons hot brewed coffee
1 cup sifted confectioners' sugar	Pinch of salt
1 tablespoon unsweetened cocoa powder	1/4 teaspoon vanilla
	About 5 dozen walnut halves

Combine sugar and cocoa in medium-size bowl. Stir, mashing out any lumps in cocoa. Add oil; beat with electric mixer or wooden spoon until fluffy. Beat in egg.

On a large square of waxed paper, combine flour, baking powder, baking soda and salt. Add flour mixture alternately with buttermilk in four or five portions to sugar mixture. Stir in vanilla and chopped walnuts.

Drop dough by rounded teaspoonfuls onto greased baking sheets. Bake in a preheated 400-degree oven 8 to 10 minutes, or until tops hold slight dent when pressed. Remove from pans and let cool thoroughly on wire racks.

For Mocha Frosting: In small bowl, work butter until creamy, then gradually work in confectioners' sugar and cocoa. Stir in coffee, salt and vanilla. If too stiff, add a bit more coffee.

Spread Mocha Frosting on cooled cookies. Place a walnut half on each cookie.

Whole Wheat Pineapple Drops

Jeanne Voltz
Cookbook Author, Pittsboro, North Carolina

This reminds me of the cookies that my mother served us with milk when we came home from school. They are sturdy, no-nonsense treats for hungry school children. To recall those easier times, I pour the milk from my grandmother's pale blue pitcher with a windmill on the side for an afternoon cookie break.

Makes about 2-1/2 dozen cookies

1 can (8 ounces) crushed pineapple in juice	1 egg
1/2 cup golden raisins	1 cup all-purpose or unbleached flour
1/3 cup vegetable oil (canola or corn oil recommended)	1 cup whole wheat flour
	1 teaspoon baking powder
3/4 cup granulated sugar	1/2 teaspoon baking soda
	2 teaspoons grated lemon peel

Pour pineapple with its juice into sieve over small bowl. Drain and press pineapple lightly with back of spoon to extract most of the juice. Pour 2 tablespoons of the pineapple juice over raisins; mix lightly and let stand while mixing dough. Save remaining juice for another use.

In a large mixing bowl with an electric mixer, beat oil and sugar until fluffy. Add egg; beat until well mixed. Stir in drained pineapple. Stir in flours, 1/2 cup at a time, adding baking powder and baking soda with second addition. Gently stir in raisin mixture and lemon peel.

Drop dough by rounded teaspoonfuls onto ungreased baking sheets. Bake in a preheated 375-degree oven 15 to 16 minutes, or until tops of cookies hold a small dent when pressed lightly. Transfer to racks to cool.

Molded Cookies

Including balls, twists, crescents and other handmade shapes

Aggression Cookies

Barbara Mihalevich Arciero
Food Writer, *The Times,* Shreveport, Louisiana

When I was a student at the University of Missouri, I spent a semester working in a preschool. That's where I discovered Aggression Cookies, a not-so-unique cookie with a unique name. These cookies, I discovered, offer a socially acceptable way for youngsters to let off steam and to make a tasty snack at the same time. The dough is stiff, so children can mash, knead, squeeze and pound it to their hearts' content without inflicting any damage. Children don't need to know the name of these cookies; just tell them you've got a special cookie for them to make.

Makes about 7 dozen cookies

1-1/2 cups firmly packed brown sugar
1-1/2 cups butter or margarine, softened
3 cups old-fashioned or quick-cooking rolled oats, uncooked

1-1/2 teaspoons baking soda
1-1/2 cups all-purpose flour
Granulated sugar

Combine brown sugar, butter, oats, baking soda and flour in a large mixing bowl. Mash, knead, squeeze and pound ingredients to make a dough.

Form dough into small balls. Put balls on ungreased baking sheets. Grease the bottom of a small glass or jar; dip into granulated sugar and use to flatten balls.

Bake in a preheated 350-degree oven about 15 minutes, or until done. Transfer to racks to cool.

Butter Mix Cookies

Beth Whitley Duke
Food Editor, *Amarillo Globe-News,* Amarillo, Texas

This recipe makes a lot, so it is a favorite when you need to make a lot of cookies for a crowd. The recipe originally called for a white or yellow cake mix, but you can vary the results by using a spice or chocolate cake mix. Lemon or cherry cake mixes add color and flavor to the basic recipe.

Makes 6 to 8 dozen cookies

1/3 cup butter
1/2 cup solid vegetable
 shortening
2 egg yolks

1/2 teaspoon vanilla
1 box (18-1/2 ounces) white or
 yellow cake mix
1/2 cup chopped nuts (optional)

In a large mixing bowl with an electric mixer on low speed or with a wire whisk, combine butter, shortening, egg yolks and vanilla. Blend in dry cake mix, adding about one-third at a time. If dough seems dry, add 1 to 1-1/2 teaspoons water. Stir in nuts, if desired.

Form small teaspoonfuls of dough into balls. Place balls on ungreased baking sheets. Bake in a preheated 375-degree oven 8 to 10 minutes, or until done. Let cool on wire racks. Allow baking sheet to cool thoroughly between batches.

Chocolate-Vanilla Marbled Cookies

Rita Barrett

Vice President, International Cookbook Services, White Plains, New York

This recipe is for a vanilla cookie with chocolate marbling. You can change the cookie to a chocolate cookie with vanilla marbling by adding the chocolate to the larger portion of dough instead of the smaller portion of dough. The amount of marbling that will be visible in the cookie depends on how much you knead the dough.

Makes about 5 dozen cookies

1 egg
1/2 cup unsalted butter, softened
1 teaspoon almond extract
1 package (17-1/4 ounces) vanilla or golden cake mix

1/4 cup plus 1 tablespoon all-purpose flour, divided
2 tablespoons unsweetened cocoa powder
4 teaspoons boiling water

In a medium bowl with an electric mixer on medium speed, beat egg, butter and almond extract until light and fluffy. Add dry cake mix and 1/4 cup flour. Stir with a wooden spoon to make a soft dough.

Remove one-third of the dough and place in a separate bowl. Dissolve cocoa in boiling water. Add cocoa and remaining 1 tablespoon flour to the portion of dough in separate bowl. Stir until well combined. This makes the chocolate dough.

Add chocolate dough to remaining two-thirds of plain dough; knead gently about 10 to 12 strokes to make marbled dough. Divide dough in half; shape each half into a 7-inch log. Wrap logs separately in waxed paper or plastic wrap; refrigerate at least 2 hours.

Cut each log into 1/4-inch thick slices. Place slices, about 1-1/2 inches apart, on ungreased baking sheets.

Bake in a preheated 375-degree oven 10 to 12 minutes, or until edges are golden. Remove from baking sheets and let cool completely on wire racks.

Cinnamon Letters

Barbara Bloch
President, International Cookbook Services, White Plains, New York

You can shape these cookies any way you like: circles, knots or triangles. Best of all, you can make the letters of the alphabet. This cookie is fun to make with children and fun to make for them. When my children were very young, birthday party treats for their guests were always little baskets filled with cookies that spelled the name of each guest.

Makes about 4 dozen cookies

1-1/2 cups plus 3 tablespoons granulated sugar, divided
1 cup unsalted butter, softened
2 eggs
3 cups all-purpose flour

2 teaspoons baking powder
1 teaspoon baking soda
1/2 teaspoon salt
2 teaspoons ground cinnamon, divided

In a large mixing bowl with an electric mixer on medium speed, beat 1-1/2 cups sugar and butter until light and fluffy. Add eggs; beat until blended. Sift flour, baking powder, baking soda, salt and 1/2 teaspoon cinnamon over butter mixture. Mix with wooden spoon to make stiff dough. Cover bowl and refrigerate at least 2 hours.

Divide dough into 48 walnut-sized pieces. Shape each piece of dough into a 5- to 6-inch-long rope. Shape ropes into letters, circles, knots, triangles or whatever shape you want. Place on greased baking sheets, leaving about 2 inches between cookies.

In a small bowl, combine remaining 3 tablespoons sugar and remaining 1-1/2 teaspoons cinnamon. Sprinkle cinnamon-sugar mixture over cookies.

Bake in a preheated 350-degree oven 13 to 15 minutes, or until golden brown. Remove from baking sheets and let cool completely on wire racks.

Crisp and Chewy Oatmeal-Raisin Cookies

Pamela Anderson

Food Editor, *Restaurant Business,* New York, New York

These flourless oatmeal-raisin cookies are at once crisp and chewy. Toasting the oats gives the cookies a nutty flavor.

Makes 2 dozen cookies

1-1/2 cups old-fashioned rolled oats, uncooked

5-1/2 tablespoons unsalted butter, melted and cooled

1 teaspoon vanilla

1 egg

1/2 cup raisins

1/2 cup granulated sugar

1/4 cup firmly packed light brown sugar

1/8 teaspoon salt

Spread oats on a baking sheet. Toast in a preheated 350-degree oven 5 minutes, or until fragrant; set aside to cool.

In a large mixing bowl with an electric mixer on medium speed, beat butter, vanilla and egg until light and fluffy. In another large bowl, combine raisins, toasted oats, granulated sugar, brown sugar and salt. Stir in butter mixture; mix well. Refrigerate dough at least 20 minutes.

Form chilled dough into 1-inch balls; place balls, 2 inches apart, on baking sheet lined with parchment paper. Using your lightly floured palm, flatten each ball into a disk, 1-1/4 inches in diameter. Bake in a preheated 350-degree oven 15 minutes, or until edges are browned.

Let cookies cool completely on the baking sheet, then use a spatula to remove them. Cookies can be stored in an airtight container up to one week.

Crisp Indian-Spiced Sugar Cookies

Pamela Anderson

Food Editor, *Restaurant Business*, New York, New York

These crisp sugar cookies are flavored with assertive Indian spices—cardamom, ginger and cloves. You should refrigerate the dough at least six hours, but, if you are in a hurry, you can put the cookie dough in the freezer for about one hour, or until it is cold and firm but not frozen.

Makes 4 dozen cookies

1-3/4 cups all-purpose flour
2 teaspoons baking powder
1/4 teaspoon salt
1 teaspoon ground cardamom
1/2 teaspoon ground ginger
1/4 teaspoon ground cloves
1/2 cup unsalted butter, softened

1 cup plus 2 tablespoons granulated sugar, divided
1 teaspoon vanilla
1 egg
2 tablespoons milk
1 teaspoon grated lemon zest
1 tablespoon lemon juice

Mix flour, baking powder, salt, cardamom, ginger and cloves in a medium bowl; set aside.

In a large mixing bowl with an electric mixer on medium speed, beat butter until light and fluffy. Add 1 cup sugar; beat until smooth. Beat in vanilla, egg and milk. Beat in lemon zest and lemon juice. With mixer on low speed, gradually beat in reserved flour mixture.

Transfer dough to an 18-inch square of parchment paper; shape dough into a 12- by 2-inch log. Wrap dough and refrigerate about 6 hours, or until firm. (At this point, the dough can be refrigerated up to 3 days.)

Cut log into 1/4-inch thick slices. Place slices, 2 inches apart, on a cookie sheet lined with parchment paper. Sprinkle slices with remaining 2 tablespoons sugar.

Bake in a preheated 375-degree oven 10 to 13 minutes, or until cookie edges are lightly browned. Let cookies cool slightly on the baking sheet, then use a spatula to transfer them to a wire rack to cool completely. Cookies can be stored in an airtight container up to one week.

Crispy Molasses Sugar Cookies

Evelyn Cairns

Food Editor, *The News-Herald Newspapers,* Southgate, Michigan

The spicy aroma of freshly baked molasses cookies brings back memories of baking sessions with a loving grandmother whose enthusiasm for creating delectables was contagious. She died at 101 and left a legacy of wonderful recipes, including her favorite version of molasses sugar cookies. I enjoyed these cookies with a glass of milk while grandmother liked them with a cup of hot lemon tea.

Makes 5 to 6 dozen cookies

3/4 cup solid vegetable
   shortening
1 cup granulated sugar
1/4 cup molasses (light or dark)
1 egg
2 cups sifted all-purpose flour
2 teaspoons baking soda

1/2 teaspoon ground cloves
1/2 teaspoon ground ginger
1 teaspoon ground cinnamon
1/2 teaspoon salt
Additional granulated sugar,
   for rolling

Melt shortening in a 3-quart saucepan over low heat. Remove from heat and let cool. Add sugar, molasses and egg; beat well.

Sift together flour, baking soda, cloves, ginger, cinnamon and salt. Add flour mixture to molasses mixture; mix well. Refrigerate dough 1 to 2 hours.

Form chilled dough into 1-inch balls, then roll balls in granulated sugar. Place balls, 2 inches apart, on greased baking sheets. Bake in a preheated 375-degree oven 8 to 10 minutes, or until done.

Espresso Fudge Cups

Marlene Sorosky
Free-lance Writer, Hunt Valley, Maryland

When testing recipes for one of my cookbooks, I had a brainstorm. Wouldn't it be great to create a cookie with the taste and texture of a rich, fudgey brownie in a fancier shape? It must have taken me 20 attempts before these moist, chocolatey cushions reached my expectations. I even worked out variations, substituting grated orange peel or seedless raspberry jam for the coffee powder, and almonds or macadamias for the pecans. Imagine my surprise when I received the first copy of the cookbook and these were deleted because it had too many recipes.

Makes 24 cookies

1/2 cup unsalted butter
1/2 cup semisweet chocolate
   morsels
2 eggs
1/2 cup all-purpose flour

1 teaspoon instant espresso or
   coffee granules
3/4 cup granulated sugar
1/2 cup chopped pecans
24 pecan halves

In a medium-size, microwave-safe bowl or the top of double boiler over simmering water, melt butter and chocolate; stir until smooth. Let cool slightly. Whisk in eggs. Stir in flour, coffee powder and sugar; mix well. Stir in chopped pecans.

Line 24 (1-3/4-inch diameter) mini-muffin tins with paper muffin cups. Spoon batter into cups, filling them almost to the top. Place a pecan half on top of each.

Bake in the center of a preheated 350-degree oven 18 to 20 minutes, or until the tops are set and a toothpick inserted in the center comes out clean. Let cool 2 to 3 minutes, then remove to rack to finish cooling.

Note: The cups can be stored in an airtight container for several days or frozen.

Hazelnut Raspberry Cream Cheese Gems

Laura J. Barton
Free-lance Writer, Portland, Oregon

High on my list of favorite Northwest foods are raspberries and hazelnuts. Combining them is heavenly and has inspired many delicious recipes, including this one.

Makes 30 cookies

1/2 cup butter, softened
1 package (3 ounces) cream cheese, softened
1 egg, separated
1 teaspoon vanilla
1 teaspoon grated lemon peel

1 cup confectioners' sugar
1 cup all-purpose flour
1 cup finely chopped hazelnuts (filberts)
Raspberry jam

In a large mixing bowl with an electric mixer, beat butter, cream cheese, egg yolk, vanilla and lemon peel until well blended. Mix in confectioners' sugar, then flour to make a stiff dough.

Refrigerate dough. Shape chilled dough into 30 small balls. Beat egg white until foamy. Dip balls in egg white, then roll in nuts. Place balls on lightly greased baking sheets. Press an indentation into the center of each ball; fill with a little raspberry jam.

Bake in a preheated 350-degree oven 10 to 15 minutes, or until cookies begin to brown on the bottom. Let cool. Store in an airtight container.

Health Cookies

Barbara Burklo
Food Editor (Retired), *Santa Cruz Sentinel,* Santa Cruz, California

My mother, Flora Deemy, made these chewy cookies during the years when I was growing up in Vancouver, Washington. I can smell them yet, baking in the old oven in her tiny kitchen. In turn, I baked them for our four children when they were growing up—and I still enjoy preparing these nutritious treats.

Makes 3 to 4 dozen cookies

1 cup granulated sugar
1 cup firmly packed brown sugar
1 cup solid vegetable shortening
2 eggs
1 tablespoon vanilla
2 cups all-purpose flour
1 teaspoon baking soda
1/2 teaspoon baking powder
1 teaspoon salt
1 cup old-fashioned or quick-cooking rolled oats, uncooked
1 cup all-bran cereal or bran flakes
1 cup corn flakes
1 cup shredded coconut
Walnut halves (optional)

In a large mixing bowl with an electric mixer on medium speed, beat granulated sugar, brown sugar and shortening until light and fluffy. Add eggs and vanilla; mix well.

Sift flour, baking soda, baking powder and salt into another bowl. Add flour mixture to sugar mixture; mix well with a wooden spoon. Add oats, bran cereal, corn flakes and coconut; mix well (fingers work best at this point).

Roll cookie dough between palms to form small, walnut-size or slightly larger balls. Place balls on well-greased baking sheets; flatten balls with tines of a fork. If desired, press walnut half in center of each.

Bake in a preheated 350-degree oven 12 to 15 minutes, or until done. Transfer cookies to wire racks to cool.

Note: These cookies freeze well in tightly covered containers.

Lemon Refrigerator Cookies

Jeanne Voltz
Cookbook Author, Pittsboro, North Carolina

These delicately flavored wafers taste wonderful with iced tea or lemonade on a summer afternoon. Ice box cookies remind me of my Grandmother Appleton. She adopted every food fad that came down the pike back when "trends" meant cooking and new recipes, not restaurant hopping. After she bought her first electric refrigerator, she always kept a roll of cookie dough in it to slice and bake when a grandchild needed comfort food.

Makes 4 dozen cookies

1/2 cup butter or margarine, softened
1/2 cup granulated sugar
1 egg
1 tablespoon lemon juice
2 teaspoons grated lemon peel

1-1/2 cups all-purpose or unbleached flour
1/4 teaspoon salt
Additional granulated sugar, for sprinkling (optional)

In a medium mixing bowl with an electric mixer, beat butter and sugar until fluffy. Add egg; beat until smooth. Beat in lemon juice and lemon peel. Stir in flour and salt.

Divide dough in half and place each half on a large square of waxed paper. Knead lightly to blend thoroughly. Shape each half into a roll about 1-1/2 inches in diameter. Wrap rolls in waxed paper, twisting ends of rolls closed. Refrigerate at least 4 hours. Dough can be kept up to one week in refrigerator.

With a sharp knife, cut rolls into 1/8-inch thick slices. Place slices on ungreased baking sheets. If desired, sprinkle sugar on slices.

Bake in a preheated 400-degree oven 8 to 10 minutes, or just until edges turn brown. Remove from pans and let cool on wire racks.

Lemon Tarts

Anne Byrn

Food Writer, *Atlanta Journal-Constitution*, Atlanta, Georgia

Each year the Atlanta Speech School Guild stages a gala at Neiman-Marcus to raise funds for the school, which treats people with hearing and speech difficulties. From the spread of desserts on hand, these tarts are my favorite. They're a nice addition to a dessert buffet and can be toted with ease to a picnic. They also freeze nicely.

Makes about 2 dozen tarts

Filling:

2 eggs
2 egg yolks
1 cup granulated sugar
Juice of 2 lemons
Grated peel of 2 lemons
1/2 cup unsalted butter or margarine

Pastry Shells:

1 cup all-purpose flour
1 package (3 ounces) cream cheese, softened
1/2 cup unsalted butter, softened

For Filling: Place eggs and egg yolks in the top of a double boiler over simmering water. Beat gently until whites and yolks are mixed well. Add sugar, lemon juice and lemon peel; mix well. Place butter on top of mixture. Cook over low heat, stirring, 10 to 12 minutes, or until butter melts and mixture is the consistency of mayonnaise. Set aside to cool.

For Pastry Shells: Blend flour, cream cheese and butter with pastry blender or in food processor. Refrigerate dough 30 minutes. Roll dough into balls the size of a large marble. Place one ball in each cup of a greased mini-muffin tin. Press ball into cup, making sure dough comes all the way to the top of the cup. Prick dough with a fork. Bake in a preheated 325-degree oven about 20 minutes. Let shells cool, then fill with cooled filling.

Nutty-Berry Thumbprints

Barbara Bloch
President, International Cookbook Services, White Plains, New York

*Several years ago, my husband invited an old college
friend to visit us. He was a man who had several degrees
and had gained enormous recognition in his field for
research and academic accomplishments. I served these
cookies with ice cream, and I still remember the quizzi-
cal expression on his face when he saw them. I asked
him if anything was wrong. He shook his head and said,
"No, nothing is wrong. I just can't figure out how you
got the jam inside the cookies!"*

Makes about 5 dozen cookies

2 cups granulated sugar
1-1/2 cups unsalted butter, softened
3 eggs
2 teaspoons vanilla
4 cups all-purpose flour
1 teaspoon baking soda
1/2 teaspoon salt

1 egg white beaten with 1 tablespoon water
3/4 cup finely chopped almonds, hazelnuts (filberts) or macadamia nuts
About 1/2 cup strawberry, raspberry, blueberry or blackberry jam

In a large mixing bowl with an electric mixer on medium speed, beat sugar and butter until light and fluffy. Add eggs and vanilla; beat until blended. Combine flour, baking soda, and salt; add to butter mixture and beat until well combined. Cover bowl and refrigerate at least 2 hours.

Shape dough into slightly flattened walnut-size balls. Dip bottom of each ball into beaten egg white and then into chopped nuts. Place balls, nut-side up, on ungreased baking sheets, leaving about 2 inches between balls. Make a hollow in center of each ball with thumb or end of wooden spoon. Fill hollows with jam.

Bake in a preheated 350-degree oven 10 to 12 minutes, or until golden. Let cool on baking sheets 5 minutes. Transfer to wire racks to cool completely.

Peanut Brittle-Cream Cheese Cookies

Barbara Bloch
President, International Cookbook Services, White Plains, New York

*My husband has a passion for peanut brittle in any
and every form, so it is not surprising that these cookies
are one of his favorites. I make them for him on special
occasions and sometimes "just because."*

Makes about 4 dozen cookies

1 cup unsalted butter, softened
1 package (3 ounces) cream
  cheese, softened
1 cup granulated sugar
1 egg
1 teaspoon vanilla or almond
  extract

1-1/2 cups crushed peanut brittle
2-1/3 cups all-purpose flour
1/2 teaspoon baking soda
Additional granulated sugar,
  for sprinkling

In a medium bowl with an electric mixer on medium speed, beat butter, cream cheese and sugar until light and fluffy. Add egg and vanilla; beat until blended. Fold in peanut brittle. Add flour and baking soda; stir with a wooden spoon to make a soft dough. Cover bowl and refrigerate at least 3 hours.

Shape dough into 1-inch balls. Place balls, about 2 inches apart, on ungreased baking sheets. Dip tines of fork into flour and press tines across tops of cookies to flatten; press again in opposite direction. Sprinkle cookies with granulated sugar.

Bake in a preheated 350-degree oven 10 to 12 minutes, or just until cookies are golden. Remove from baking sheets and let cool completely on wire racks.

Peanut Butter Cookies

Doris Reynolds

Food Columnist, *Naples Daily News,* Naples, Florida

The best cook I ever knew was Alta Riley of Naples, Florida, who operated one of the most creative catering services I've ever encountered. Riley, who died in 1989, knew how to cook everything well — from soup to extravagant pastries. I once hired her to do a Fourth of July party and for dessert she served homemade lemon ice cream and a large batch of Peanut Butter Cookies. Because 1990 marked the 100th anniversary of peanut butter, it is only fitting that I share the best recipe I have for this typical American treat.

Makes 5 to 6 dozen cookies

1/2 cup butter or margarine	2 eggs, well beaten
1/4 teaspoon salt	1 tablespoon milk
1 cup chunky peanut butter	1 cup sifted all-purpose flour
3/4 cup granulated sugar	1/4 teaspoon baking soda
3/4 cup firmly packed brown sugar	1/4 teaspoon ground ginger

In a large bowl with an electric mixer, beat butter, salt and peanut butter until well blended. Add sugar, brown sugar, eggs and milk; mix well.

Sift flour, baking soda and ginger into a separate bowl. Gradually stir flour mixture into peanut butter mixture. With your hands, roll the dough into small balls. Place balls on ungreased baking sheets. Flatten balls with the tines of a fork, making a criss-cross pattern.

Bake in a preheated 325-degree oven 15 to 20 minutes, or until done. Transfer to wire racks to cool.

Peanut Butter Sandies

Pamela Anderson
Food Editor, *Restaurant Business,* New York, New York

Confectioners' sugar gives these Peanut Butter Sandies that melt-in-your-mouth quality. You can substitute almond, pistachio or cashew butter and the corresponding nut for the peanut butter and chopped peanuts.

Makes 4 dozen cookies

2 cups all-purpose flour
1 teaspoon baking powder
1/2 teaspoon baking soda
1/4 teaspoon salt
7/8 cup (1-3/4 sticks) unsalted
  butter, softened
1/2 cup creamy peanut butter
1 cup confectioners' sugar,
  sifted

1/2 cup firmly packed light
  brown sugar
1-1/2 teaspoons vanilla
1 egg
1/2 cup coarsely chopped
  peanuts

In a large bowl, combine flour, baking powder, baking soda and salt; set aside.

In a large mixing bowl with an electric mixer on medium speed, beat butter and peanut butter until light and fluffy. Add confectioners' sugar and brown sugar; beat on medium speed until smooth. Beat in vanilla and egg. With mixer on low speed, gradually beat in reserved flour mixture. Fold in peanuts by hand.

Form dough into 1-1/4-inch balls. Place balls, 2 inches apart, on baking sheet lined with parchment paper. Using your lightly floured palm, flatten each ball into a disk, 1-1/2 inches in diameter. Bake in a preheated 350-degree oven about 10 minutes, or until edges are lightly browned.

Let cookies cool slightly on baking sheet, then use a spatula to transfer cookies to a wire rack; let cool completely. Cookies can be stored in an airtight container up to one week.

Pecan Fingers

Sally Cappon

Food Writer, *Santa Barbara News-Press,* Santa Barbara, California

My mother was a working mother 50 years before her time. When I was growing up in Milwaukee, my friends' mothers baked 11 different kinds of cookies every Christmas. My mother baked one kind — Pecan Fingers. She took them everywhere cookies were called for and they were wonderfully received. An easy cookie with intergenerational appeal, they're also on my kids' "wish list" every Christmas. I always double the recipe.

Makes 3 to 4 dozen cookies

1 cup butter
1/4 cup confectioners' sugar
1 teaspoon vanilla
1 tablespoon water
2 cups all-purpose flour

1/4 teaspoon salt
2 cups grated pecans
Additional confectioners'
   sugar, for rolling

In a medium mixing bowl with an electric mixer on medium speed, beat butter until creamy. Add confectioners' sugar, vanilla and water; mix well. Add flour, salt and pecans. Refrigerate dough about 1 hour.

Form chilled dough into small rolls about the size of a little finger. Place rolls on greased baking sheets. Bake in a preheated 350-degree oven 12 to 15 minutes, or until lightly browned. (The original recipe called for baking rolls in a preheated 250-degree oven 1 hour. Either way works.) While cookies are still warm, roll them in confectioners' sugar.

Tea Tots

Narcisse S. Cadgène
Free-lance Writer, New York, New York

These light little cookies are wonderfully easy, and the small amount of dough can be baked on one sheet. Because they're so light, they are a perfect choice to serve as an after-lunch cookie or for tea. They're especially convenient if you're watching your weight, because you won't have a couple of dozen left over that you'll eat by yourself when your guests are gone!

Makes 24 to 30 cookies

6 tablespoons butter
1/3 cup granulated sugar
1 to 2 egg yolks

1/4 teaspoon finely grated lemon zest
1 cup all-purpose flour

With an electric mixer, beat butter and sugar until light. Beat in egg yolk (2 yolks will make a slightly richer cookie) and lemon zest. Stir in flour with a spoon or rubber spatula. Refrigerate dough.

Roll chilled dough into 1-inch balls. Place balls on greased baking sheet. Slightly flatten each ball with your thumb or the bottom of a glass. Bake in a preheated 375-degree oven 10 to 12 minutes, or until edges brown. Let cool on a rack.

Snickerdoodles

Laura J. Barton
Free-lance Writer, Portland, Oregon

Because both of my parents worked outside the home, homemade cookies were a rare treat in our house. One type of homemade cookie my mother made occasionally, and that I remember best, was this cookie. Maybe it was the funny name, or the cinnamon-y smell as they came out of the oven, but now whenever I'm in a nostalgic mood, I bake a batch of Snickerdoodles.

Makes about 6 dozen cookies

1/2 cup butter, softened
1/2 cup solid vegetable
  shortening
1-1/2 cups plus 2 tablespoons
  granulated sugar, divided
2 eggs

2-3/4 cups all-purpose flour
2 teaspoons cream of tartar
1 teaspoon baking soda
1/4 teaspoon salt
2 teaspoons ground cinnamon

In a large mixing bowl with an electric mixer, beat butter, shortening, 1-1/2 cups sugar and eggs until well mixed. Blend in flour, cream of tartar, baking soda and salt.

Shape dough by rounded teaspoonfuls into balls. Combine cinnamon and remaining 2 tablespoons sugar. Roll balls in cinnamon-sugar mixture. Place balls, 2 inches apart, on ungreased baking sheets.

Bake in a preheated 400-degree oven 8 to 10 minutes, or until set. Remove from baking sheets; let cool on wire racks.

Vienna Sugar Cookies

Beverly Bundy

Food Editor, *Fort Worth Star-Telegram,* Fort Worth, Texas

This recipe was requested in The Fort Worth Star-Telegram's *reader exchange column. Several contributors wrote to say that these cookies had helped curb morning sickness during pregnancy. Hey, whatever works.*

Makes 3 to 4 dozen cookies

1 package active dry yeast
1/2 cup lukewarm water
1 cup butter

2 cups all-purpose flour
1 cup granulated sugar

Dissolve yeast in lukewarm water. In a large mixing bowl with an electric mixer, beat butter until creamy. Gradually add flour, blending well. Add yeast mixture; blend well. Refrigerate dough until chilled.

Put sugar on a large piece of waxed paper. Pinch off pieces of chilled dough the size of small walnuts and shape into balls. Working with one ball of dough at a time, press ball flat into sugar until dough is thin. Keep flipping dough over and pressing it into sugar, until it is the size of a flat doughnut. Place on ungreased baking sheets.

Bake in a preheated 375-degree oven 10 to 15 minutes, or until very lightly browned. Transfer to racks to cool.

Vivian's Dainties

Jim Hillibish

Food Editor, *The Repository*, Canton, Ohio

This recipe turned up in a dusty wooden box at a garage sale in Canton, Ohio. It turned out to be much more valuable than the box, which cost 35 cents.

Vivian, whoever she is, came up with a recipe similar to what some call Russian Tea Balls. She improved upon it, adding pecans, which offer a nutty-sweet flavor, as opposed to the usual walnuts.

Be forewarned about the baking. These cookies burn exceptionally fast. Keep an eye on them, and Vivian will reward you, generously.

Makes about 2 dozen cookies

1 cup butter
1/2 cup confectioners' sugar
2-1/4 cups all-purpose flour
1 teaspoon salt

1 teaspoon vanilla
1 cup chopped pecans
Additional confectioners' sugar, for rolling

In a mixing bowl with an electric mixer, cream butter and confectioners' sugar. Gradually beat in flour, salt and vanilla. Mix well. Stir in pecans. Roll dough into 3/4-inch balls. Place balls on greased baking sheets (preferably black metal). Bake in a preheated 400-degree oven 15 minutes, or until done.

While cookies are still warm, roll in confectioners' sugar. Let cool on paper towels.

Rolled Cookies

Including those made with a rolling pin, cookie cutter, or other special equipment, such as pastry bags, cookie presses and cookie irons

Almond Pizzelles

Laura J. Barton
Free-lance Writer, Portland, Oregon

Pizzelles have their origins in Italy. I have always been intrigued by their lacy patterns. I love to make pizzelles in the summertime because they go so well with fresh fruit combinations and ice cream or sorbets. Because they are made in an iron, these cookies do not require the use of an oven, which heats up the kitchen. The pizzelle recipe I use the most is adapted from one that came with my electric pizzelle iron.

Makes approximately 30 (5-inch) pizzelles

1/2 cup butter	1 teaspoon vanilla
3 eggs	1-3/4 cups all-purpose flour
3/4 cup granulated sugar	2 teaspoons baking powder
2 teaspoons almond extract	

In a small saucepan, melt butter; let cool slightly.

In a medium mixing bowl, beat eggs; gradually add sugar, beating until smooth. Add melted butter, almond extract and vanilla; mix well. Add flour and baking powder; stir until blended. Dough will be sticky enough to be dropped by a spoon.

Heat the pizzelle iron, then drop a rounded teaspoon of batter in the center of each pizzelle grid; bake until steaming stops and the pizzelles are golden (approximately 30 to 60 seconds, depending upon size of the pizzelle and desired crispness). Remove each pizzelle with a fork or spatula, and let cool on a rack. Store in an airtight container.

Apricot Cookie Rolls

Suzanne Hall
Food Editor, *The Chattanooga Times*, Chattanooga, Tennessee

My mother and I both love coconut and apricots, so I was delighted when, while attending a holiday cookie swap, I was introduced to a cookie which uses both. Because the dough requires at least 4 hours chilling time, I usually start these the night before. Then the next morning all I have to do is make the filling, put the cookies together and bake them.

Makes about 5 dozen cookies

1 cup butter, softened	1/2 cup shredded coconut
1 cup dairy sour cream	1/2 cup apricot preserves
1/2 teaspoon salt	1/4 cup finely chopped walnuts
2 cups all-purpose flour	Confectioners' sugar (optional)

In a mixing bowl with an electric mixer, beat butter until fluffy. Add sour cream and salt, mixing well. Gradually add flour, mixing well after each addition. Divide dough into four parts; wrap each part in foil and refrigerate at least 4 hours, or overnight.

Combine coconut, apricot preserves and walnuts; mix well.

Remove chilled dough from refrigerator, one piece at a time. Keep remaining dough in refrigerator until ready to use. Roll dough 1/8-inch thick on well-floured surface. (Dough will be slightly soft.) Cut rolled dough into 2-1/2-inch squares; spread each square with 1/2 teaspoon coconut mixture. Starting with a corner, carefully roll up each square. Moisten opposite edges and press to seal. Place rolls on greased baking sheets, seam-side up. Repeat with remaining dough and coconut mixture.

Bake in a preheated 350-degree oven 16 to 18 minutes, or until tips are lightly browned. Remove from baking sheets; let cool slightly, then sprinkle with confectioners' sugar, if desired.

Apricot Pockets

Louise F. Dodd

Food Editor, *Courier Herald,* Dublin, Georgia

*This recipe was given to me by an artistic neighbor
who also was a wonderful cook. Her rendition of this
was so perfect and so precise that it almost makes the
amateur artist give up in defeat. Keep working with it,
though, and you will find that you will soon master the
art of making the pocketbooks with exact precision.
Even if you don't, they are quite delicious.*

Makes about 30 cookies

1/2 cup butter or margarine
4 ounces sharp Cheddar cheese, grated (1 cup)
1-1/3 cups sifted all-purpose flour

2 tablespoons cold water
1 cup pitted, chopped dried apricots
1 cup granulated sugar

In a mixing bowl with an electric mixer, beat butter and cheese until light. Blend in the sifted flour. Add water; mix well. Refrigerate dough several hours.

Cook apricots in a small amount of water until soft. Drain off liquid. Stir sugar into hot apricots. Cook and stir until mixture boils and becomes smooth. Remove from heat and let cool.

Divide chilled dough into two equal parts. Roll each half with a rolling pin on a floured surface until dough reaches about 10 inches in diameter. Cut with a biscuit cutter into 2- or 3-inch rounds. Place 1 teaspoon apricot mixture on each round; fold over and seal with the tines of a fork, mashing the edges together. Place on ungreased baking sheets.

Bake in a preheated 375-degree oven 8 to 10 minutes, or until done. Remove from the oven and let cool on racks. Serve warm or at room temperature. If you want extreme decadence, you could top them with a little whipped cream.

Bitter-Chocolate Biscuits

Lorrie Guttman

Food Editor, *Tallahassee Democrat,* Tallahassee, Florida

My husband likes chocolate, the darker the better. So when, as a newlywed some 20 years ago, I saw this recipe in a magazine, I saved it. These cookies are indeed bitter, but they go well with ice cream as a sweet complement. Their dark-brown color makes a striking presentation with vanilla or another light-colored ice cream.

Makes about 4 dozen cookies

1/2 cup butter, softened
1 cup granulated sugar
Dash of salt
1 egg
4 squares (1 ounce each) unsweetened chocolate

1-1/2 to 2 cups all-purpose flour
1 teaspoon vanilla

In a mixing bowl with an electric mixer, beat butter and sugar until light. Add salt and egg; beat until fluffy.

Melt chocolate over hot water or very low heat. Add melted chocolate to butter mixture; blend well. Add flour and vanilla, using enough flour to keep the dough from being sticky; mix well. Refrigerate until dough is firm enough to roll, about 1 hour.

On a floured surface with a floured rolling pin, roll small amounts of dough at a time to 1/4-inch thickness. Cut with a round 1-1/2- to 2-inch cookie cutter and place, 1 inch apart, on ungreased baking sheets.

Bake in a preheated 350-degree oven about 7 minutes, or until done. Remove to wire racks to cool, then store in airtight containers.

Cherry-Filled Cookies

Carole Currie

Lifestyle Editor, *Asheville Citizen*, Asheville, North Carolina

On the morning my daughter was to bake cookies for a Girl Scout cookie competition, a friend with car trouble asked me to pick her up 50 miles from home. By the time I returned home, the dough was chilled but the baking project had to be hurried up. We substituted a jar of cherry preserves for the cooked fruit filling we had planned to make, and added a touch of almond flavoring to bring out the cherry flavor. The end result was delicious and my daughter won first prize.

Makes 4-1/2 dozen cookies

1/2 cup solid vegetable shortening
1 cup granulated sugar
2 eggs
1/2 teaspoon vanilla
2-1/2 cups all-purpose flour

1/4 teaspoon baking soda
1/2 teaspoon salt
1/2 teaspoon almond extract
1 jar (about 12 ounces) cherry preserves

In a mixing bowl with an electric mixer, beat shortening, sugar and eggs until light and fluffy. Stir in vanilla. Combine flour, baking soda and salt; add to shortening mixture, blending well. Refrigerate dough at least 1 hour, or overnight.

Roll chilled dough on a floured surface to 1/16-inch thickness. Cut with a 2-1/2-inch round cookie cutter. For a pretty effect, cut the center out of half of the cookies with a tiny decorative cutter or a doughnut cutter; these will be the top pieces. Place the bottom pieces on lightly greased baking sheets.

Add almond extract to cherry preserves; mix well. Spread a rounded teaspoonful of preserves on each bottom piece, but do not spread to edges. Cover with top pieces. Press edges together with floured tines of fork or fingertips.

Bake in a preheated 400-degree oven 8 to 10 minutes, or until delicately browned. Remove to racks to cool.

Note: Other flavors of preserves and flavorings can be used. For instance, substitute orange marmalade for cherry preserves and use lemon flavoring instead of almond extract.

Chocolate Wafers

Jim Hillibish

Food Editor, *The Repository*, Canton, Ohio

Here's an English cookie that stands on its own but doesn't mind some company. These light wafers are excellent alongside vanilla ice cream or fresh fruit. They make a perfect garnish for lightly sugared strawberries or raspberries.

The problem here is keeping enough around to make dessert. Chocolate lovers have a tendency to devour these wafers in alarming quantities, often before they cool. This requires either making a double recipe or finding a foolproof hiding place.

Makes 5-1/2 to 6 dozen cookies

3/4 cup butter
1-1/4 cups granulated sugar
1 egg, lightly beaten
1-1/2 cups sifted all-purpose flour

3/4 cup unsweetened cocoa powder
1-1/2 teaspoons baking powder
1/4 teaspoon salt

In a large mixing bowl with an electric mixer, beat butter until smooth; gradually add sugar, mixing well after each addition. Add egg; mix well.

Sift together flour, cocoa, baking powder and salt. Add flour mixture to butter mixture; mix well.

Roll out dough on lightly floured surface to 1/8-inch thickness. Cut with floured cookie cutter into rounds no larger than 2-1/2 inches. Place on ungreased baking sheets. Bake in a preheated 400-degree oven about 8 minutes, or until done.

Cinnamon Shortbread Hearts

Anne Byrn

Food Writer, *Atlanta Journal-Constitution*, Atlanta, Georgia

No cookie is more satisfying with a cup of tea or coffee than shortbread. In this recipe, the Scottish staple is updated to include a smidgen of cinnamon. When the shortbread is baking, the scent that wafts through the house is absolutely irresistible. Pat the dough into heart-shaped molds for Valentine's Day, pack the cookies in a decorative red tin and you have just said "I love you" to someone special.

Makes about 2 dozen cookies

2 cups unsalted butter, softened
4 cups all-purpose flour
1-1/4 cups confectioners' sugar

1 teaspoon baking powder
1/2 teaspoon ground cinnamon
1/4 teaspoon salt

In a large mixing bowl, cut butter into flour with 2 knives until mixture resembles coarse crumbs. With your hands or a rubber spatula, work in confectioners' sugar, baking powder, cinnamon and salt until well mixed.

Pinch off dough and pat into lightly oiled heart-shaped, cast-iron molds or other small baking molds. Bake in a preheated 325-degree oven 45 minutes, or until golden. Let cool in molds 20 minutes, then turn out onto racks to finish cooling. Store in airtight containers.

Filled Speculaas

Joyce van Meer
Free-lance Writer, Washington, D. C.

Speculaas is a special Dutch Christmas treat. It is a spicy cookie with almonds, which is traditionally molded into the shape of Saint Nicholas. Specialty bakeries in the Netherlands still sometimes make the giant, 12-inch high Speculaas using antique, carved molds, but you don't need a special mold to make the cookies. A richer variation is this recipe, filled with almond paste.

Makes about 2 dozen cookies

1-1/2 cups all-purpose flour
1-1/2 teaspoons baking powder
10 tablespoons (2/3 cup) butter or margarine
3/4 cup plus 2 tablespoons granulated sugar
1 tablespoon ground cinnamon
1/2 teaspoon ground cloves
1/2 teaspoon freshly grated nutmeg
1 tablespoon milk
1 teaspoon lemon zest
1 package (7 ounces) almond paste
1 egg, beaten
4 tablespoons finely sliced almonds

Sift flour with baking powder. Cut butter into flour mixture. Add sugar, cinnamon, cloves, nutmeg, milk and lemon zest; mix well.

Roll out dough on a lightly floured surface into a rectangle 1/4-inch thick. Cut in half. Place half on a heavy sheet of aluminum foil, folding the edges of foil up around dough to make a shallow, fitted pan.

Roll out the almond paste to fit on top of dough. Brush top of dough in foil pan with beaten egg, then put almond paste on top. Cover with remaining half of the dough, pressing down lightly to eliminate air bubbles. Brush top with beaten egg. Scatter almond slices over the top, pressing them lightly into the dough.

Bake in a preheated 350-degree oven 40 minutes, or until done. Let cool, then cut into bars.

Old-Fashioned Ginger Cookies

Suzanne Hall
Food Editor, *The Chattanooga Times*, Chattanooga, Tennessee

Carleon Bailey is one of a growing number of Yankees who now call Chattanooga home. Although she has lived all over the world, her cooking has its roots in a small town in Pennsylvania. "My favorite aunt, in her 80s and stil! cooking, always made these cookies for us," Bailey says. "She found the recipe more than 50 years ago on the back of a package of flour."

Makes about 3 dozen cookies

1 cup granulated sugar	1 teaspoon ground nutmeg
1 cup solid vegetable shortening	1 teaspoon ground ginger
6 cups all-purpose flour	1 teaspoon ground cinnamon
2 teaspoons baking soda	1 cup molasses
1 teaspoon salt	1 cup cold brewed coffee

In a large mixing bowl with an electric mixer, beat sugar and shortening until smooth. Sift together flour, baking soda, salt, nutmeg, ginger and cinnamon. Combine molasses and coffee. Add flour mixture to shortening mixture alternately with molasses mixture. Mix well with a wooden spoon after each addition.

Refrigerate dough about 30 minutes. Roll out dough 1/2-inch thick on lightly floured surface. Cut into desired shape with 2-1/2-inch cookie cutter. Transfer to lightly greased baking sheets.

Bake in a preheated 350-degree oven 12 to 15 minutes, or until no imprint remains when cookie is lightly touched. Remove from baking sheets and let cool on racks.

Gingersnap Wafers

Pamela Anderson

Food Editor, *Restaurant Business*, New York, New York

These gingersnap cookies are an old family recipe. To make curled wafers, immediately remove hot cookies from the baking sheet with a spatula and drape the cookies over a rolling pin. To make gingersnap twists, cut rolled-out sheet of cookie dough into 3- by 1-inch rectangles and bake, following recipe instructions. Then immediately remove the hot cookies from the baking sheet with a spatula, and, holding each end of the cookie between fingertips and thumb, twist the ends in opposite directions.

Makes 3 dozen cookies

1-3/4 cups all-purpose flour
1/4 teaspoon baking soda
1/4 teaspoon ground ginger
1/8 teaspoon salt
1/4 cup unsalted butter

1/4 cup granulated sugar
6 tablespoons molasses
1/4 teaspoon white vinegar
1 tablespoon boiling water

Mix flour, baking soda, ginger and salt in a large bowl; set aside. In a small, heavy-bottomed saucepan, combine butter, sugar and molasses; bring to a boil. Cook over medium heat until syrup reaches firm-ball stage (248 degrees on a candy thermometer), about 2 minutes. Remove pan from heat; stir in vinegar and boiling water.

Immediately, pour molasses mixture over reserved flour mixture; stir with a wooden spoon until well blended. Flatten dough into a disk, wrap it in plastic wrap, then refrigerate it at least 1 hour. (The dough can be refrigerated overnight, if desired.)

Divide dough into 6 equal pieces. On a lightly floured work surface, roll 1 piece of dough to a thickness of 1/8-inch. Using a 2-inch round cookie cutter, cut out about 6 dough circles. Place cookie dough circles 1 inch apart on a baking sheet lined with parchment paper. Repeat this procedure with remaining pieces of dough and scraps.

Bake in a preheated 350-degree oven about 5 minutes, or until cookie edges are lightly browned. Let cookies cool slightly on the baking sheet, then transfer them to a rack; let cool completely. Cookies can be stored in an airtight container up to one week.

Left Bank Chocolate Macaroons

Frances Price
Food Columnist, Baltimore, Maryland

I first tasted these in a Parisian patisserie/salon de thé. I spent the next two weeks trying to pry the recipe from the proprietor, with no luck. Undaunted, I worked out this recipe, which is more than good enough to spare you a trip to Paris for the real thing.

Makes about 4 dozen macaroons, enough for 24 filled "sandwiches"

1-1/3 cups unblanched almonds
5 squares (1 ounce each) semisweet chocolate

3 egg whites, at room temperature
1 cup granulated sugar
1 teaspoon vanilla

Ganache (chocolate cream):
1/2 cup heavy cream

4 squares (1 ounce each) semisweet chocolate, coarsely grated

Process almonds in covered blender container on high speed, 1/3 cup at a time, until finely grated. (Do not run motor more than 30 seconds at a time to avoid "cooking" the oil in the almonds.) Pass grated almonds through a medium mesh sifter, returning pieces too large to pass through sifter to blender for re-processing. Set aside.

Melt chocolate in the top of a double boiler over hot water or in a microwave oven; set aside.

In a large mixing bowl with an electric mixer on medium speed, beat egg whites until foamy throughout. Increase speed to high and gradually beat in sugar, then grated almonds and vanilla; beat until stiff peaks form. By hand, gently fold in reserved melted chocolate.

On cookie sheets lined with greased parchment or waxed paper, shape dough into 1-1/2-inch rounds with pastry bag fitted with large plain tip, or drop by heaping teaspoonfuls, leaving 3 inches between each cookie. Let stand, uncovered, 8 hours, or overnight.

Bake in a preheated 300-degree oven 18 to 20 minutes, or until set but not dry. Let cool 10 minutes, then remove from paper and transfer to wire racks to finish cooling. Store in airtight containers up to a week before filling with Ganache.

When ready to assemble cookies, prepare Ganache: In a small saucepan over medium heat, bring cream to a full boil. Add chocolate, stirring vigorously with wooden spoon. Continue to heat, stirring constantly, until chocolate is melted. Remove from heat; let cool to room temperature. Beat vigorously by hand 2 minutes, or until stiff enough to hold its shape. Spread a heaping teaspoon of Ganache on each of half of the macaroons; top each with second macaroon. Serve within 8 hours of assembly.

Lemon Spritz Cookies

Barbara Bloch
President, International Cookbook Services, White Plains, New York

These cookies freeze so beautifully I usually make a big batch and keep some in the freezer. If you don't want to make so many, cut the recipe in half. "Spritz" is the German word for squirt, and my children always looked forward to helping me "squirt" these cookies through a cookie press. It is a wonderful activity for a rainy day.

Makes about 100 cookies

2-1/2 cups unsalted butter, softened
2-1/4 cups granulated sugar
6 egg yolks
1 tablespoon vanilla
1 tablespoon lemon peel
6 cups all-purpose flour

2 teaspoons baking powder
Decoration: candied red and green cherries, candied lemon peel, colored nonpareils, crystal sugar or crushed sugar cubes

In a large bowl with an electric mixer on medium speed, beat butter, sugar, egg yolks, vanilla and lemon peel until light and fluffy. Combine flour and baking powder; gradually add to butter mixture, beating until well blended.

Pack dough into cookie press. Press cookies onto ungreased baking sheets, leaving 1 inch between cookies. Change disc on cookie press periodically to make a variety of different cookie shapes. Decorate as desired.

Bake in a preheated 350-degree oven 12 to 15 minutes, or until cookies are golden. Remove from baking sheets and let cool completely on wire racks.

New England Cookies

Barbara Burklo

Food Editor (Retired), *Santa Cruz Sentinel*, Santa Cruz, California

A Minnesota minister's wife gave this cookie recipe to my mother more than 50 years ago, and it was said to be at least 150 years old then. These crisp, delicately flavored cookies call for a minimum of ingredients, are lovely when served with tea or coffee, and they freeze well.

Makes 3 to 4 dozen cookies

2/3 cup butter
1 cup plus 2 tablespoons granulated sugar, divided
2 eggs, divided

2 cups all-purpose flour
1 teaspoon water
1 teaspoon ground cinnamon
Blanched almond halves

In a mixing bowl with an electric mixer on medium speed, beat butter and 1 cup sugar until well blended. Add 1 egg; mix well. Stir in flour, mixing well. Place dough in a covered container and refrigerate 1 hour, or until thoroughly chilled.

Whisk remaining 1 egg with water; set aside.

Mix remaining 2 tablespoons sugar with cinnamon; set aside.

When dough is chilled, roll out small amounts between waxed paper, keeping remaining dough in refrigerator until used. Roll dough approximately 1/8-inch thick, then cut it into circles or other shapes with cookie cutters. Place on well-greased baking sheets. Brush each cookie with egg mixture, then sprinkle with cinnamon-sugar mixture. Press an almond half into center of each cookie.

Bake in a preheated 375-degree oven 6 to 8 minutes, or until just delicately golden. Remove from baking sheets and let cool on bread board.

When thoroughly cool, cookies can be stored in an airtight container, or frozen.

Orange Scallop Cookies

Clara Eschmann

Food Columnist, *Macon Telegraph and News,* Macon, Georgia

One of my mother's close friends always served these cookies at her parties. She had children my age, so I also was exposed to them. She gave this South Georgia recipe to Mother, who in turn gave it to me. I think these cookies are a pretty accompaniment for ice cream or puddings or on a platter for open houses or receptions.

Makes 9 dozen cookies

1 cup butter or margarine	2 teaspoons grated orange peel
1-1/4 cups granulated sugar	4 cups sifted all-purpose flour
1 egg	1 teaspoon baking powder
1 egg white	1/4 cup orange juice

In a large mixing bowl with an electric mixer, beat butter and sugar until fluffy. Beat together egg and egg white; add orange peel. Add egg mixture to butter mixture; mix well.

Combine flour and baking powder. Add flour mixture to butter mixture alternately with orange juice, mixing well after each addition.

On a floured surface with a rolling pin, roll out dough to 1/8-inch thickness. Cut with a 2-1/2-inch scalloped cutter and place on greased baking sheets. Bake in a preheated 375-degree oven for 10 to 12 minutes, or until done. Remove to cooling racks immediately.

These cookies store well in airtight containers and freeze well.

Pinwheel Cookies

June Ann Gladfelter

Managing Editor/Features, *The Express*, Easton, Pennsylvania

My mother, Minnie Gladfelter, has been making these cookies for 35 years. She adapted a recipe she spotted in a Betty Furness Westinghouse cookbook.

Pinwheel cookies are a wonderful Christmas cookie. They're also popular at bake sales.

The original recipe called for a chocolate filling, but a date filling can be substituted. I like to double the dough recipe and prepare half with chocolate filling and half with date filling.

Makes about 3 dozen cookies

1/2 cup solid vegetable shortening
1/2 cup firmly packed brown sugar
1/2 cup granulated sugar

1/2 cup smooth peanut butter
1 egg
2 cups sifted all-purpose flour
1/2 teaspoon salt
1/2 teaspoon baking soda

Chocolate Filling:
1 package (6 ounces) semisweet chocolate morsels

1 tablespoon butter

Date Filling:
1/2 pound pitted dates, cut into fourths
1/3 cup water

1/4 cup granulated sugar
1/4 cup chopped nuts

In a large mixing bowl with an electric mixer, combine shortening, brown sugar, granulated sugar and peanut butter. Add egg; beat until light and fluffy. Sift flour with salt and baking soda. Add to shortening mixture; blend well.

Roll dough into an oblong shape 1/4-inch thick. Cover dough with waxed paper or clean towel while preparing either the chocolate or the date filling.

To make Chocolate Filling: Melt chocolate morsels over hot water. Mix butter with the melted chocolate. Let cool slightly.

To make Date Filling: Cook dates, water and sugar until thick, stirring constantly. Remove from heat. Add nuts. Let cool slightly.

To assemble cookies, spread either chocolate or date filling on the rolled-out dough. Roll up like a jelly roll. Wrap in waxed paper and refrigerate several hours, or overnight.

To bake, cut roll into slices 1/4-inch thick; place slices on ungreased baking sheets. Bake in a preheated 375-degree oven 10 to 12 minutes, or until lightly browned. Remove from baking sheets immediately. Let cool on racks.

These cookies freeze well.

Soft Molasses Cookies

Betty Bernard

Food Editor, *Lake Charles American Press*, Lake Charles, Louisiana

Living in sugar cane-growing country here in South Louisiana, we have the best syrups in the world. This is an old recipe that was used a lot back in World War II days when sugar was rationed, but every country place grew a patch of cane to have syrup and molasses made at the closest mill. These are good with a glass of cold milk anytime.

Makes 4 dozen cookies

3 cups sifted all-purpose flour
1-1/2 teaspoons baking powder
1/2 teaspoon baking soda
1/2 teaspoon ground ginger
1/2 teaspoon ground cinnamon
1/4 teaspoon salt

1/2 cup solid vegetable shortening
1 cup molasses
2 tablespoons warm water
1 egg, beaten

Sift together flour, baking powder, baking soda, ginger, cinnamon and salt.

In another bowl, combine shortening, molasses, water and egg. Add shortening mixture to flour mixture; mix thoroughly. Let stand about 10 minutes.

Roll out dough on a floured surface. Cut with a cookie cutter. Place on lightly greased baking sheets. Bake in a preheated 400-degree oven about 15 minutes, or until done.

Tea Cakes

Clara Eschmann
Food Columnist, *Macon Telegraph and News,* Macon, Georgia

Tea Cakes were kept on hand in my household when I was growing up. Mama thought they were light and good for her two daughters. She also liked to keep them on hand for when friends dropped in for a cup of tea.

I can remember watching her roll them out, patiently awaiting the minute that she would hand me a small piece of dough to mold or design as she worked.

As I grew older, she let me cut them out but would always take them up and put them on the cookie sheet herself for fear my young fingers would tear them.

I truly cannot remember life without Mama's tea cakes. I'm sure hers were the best ever. As far as I know, this was her own recipe, but it could easily have been her mother's.

Makes 75 to 100 cookies, depending on size of cutter used

1/2 cup solid vegetable shortening
1/2 cup butter (do not substitute margarine)
2 cups granulated sugar
2 eggs
3-1/2 cups sifted all-purpose flour
4 teaspoons baking powder
1 teaspoon salt
1 teaspoon vanilla
Additional granulated sugar, for sprinkling

In a large mixing bowl with an electric mixer, beat together shortening, butter and sugar until fluffy. Add eggs and beat thoroughly.

Combine flour, baking powder and salt. Sift flour mixture three times. Add flour mixture to shortening mixture; mix well. Add vanilla, blending it thoroughly into dough.

Place dough on a floured surface and roll it very thin, about 1/8 inch. Cut into desired shapes with cookie cutters. Sprinkle with additional granulated sugar. Transfer to lightly greased baking sheets.

Bake in a preheated 325-degree oven 10 to 12 minutes, or until lightly brown. Let cool on racks. Store in airtight containers.

Note: These cookies will keep well for several weeks and they also freeze well.

Triple Threat Cookies

Julie Cohen

Free-lance Writer, Toronto, Ontario, Canada

This cookie dough can be used in a number of ways; hence the name triple threat. My grandmother used it for double-crust apple pie even though the pastry is heavier than pie crust. I like to use the dough to make a rolled cookie topped with cinnamon sugar. You also can make another cookie with the same dough. Just follow the instructions given here, but instead of sprinkling the dough with cinnamon sugar, spread it with jam, then roll the piece of dough into a cylinder and cut it into 1/2-inch rounds.

Makes about 6 dozen cookies

4 cups all-purpose flour	1 egg, beaten
1 cup butter	1/3 cup cold water or orange
2 cups granulated sugar, divided	juice
1 teaspoon baking powder	1 tablespoon ground cinnamon

In a large bowl, combine flour, butter, 1 cup sugar and baking powder. Rub together until mixture is consistency of cornmeal. Add egg and water. Knead until dough is satiny.

Roll out dough to 1/4-inch thickness. Combine remaining 1 cup sugar and cinnamon; sprinkle over dough. Cut dough into squares. Transfer squares to lightly greased baking sheets.

Bake in a preheated 350-degree oven 8 minutes, or until lightly browned. Let cool on racks. Store in airtight container.

Waffle Iron Brownies

Constance Hay
Free-lance Food Writer, Washington, D. C.

Here's a quick cookie to bake when you have forgotten that you volunteered to provide a treat for the classroom or the office. The recipe was given to me by a dear friend and fellow home economist, Laura Schraeder.

Different from the usual brownie, these are baked on a waffle iron instead of in the oven. Because they bake so quickly, they seem to be finished in a flash—and you are out of the kitchen with a brownie/cookie that everyone likes.

I mix the batter in the saucepan used to melt the butter, for easy cleanup. The recipe can be doubled—a good idea because these brownies disappear quickly.

Makes 2-1/2 dozen brownies

1/2 cup butter or margarine	1 tablespoon water
1/4 cup unsweetened cocoa powder	1-1/4 cups all-purpose flour
3/4 cup granulated sugar	1/4 teaspoon salt
2 eggs, well beaten	2/3 cup chopped walnuts
	Confectioners' sugar (optional)

Preheat waffle iron to medium setting. Indicator light will go out when proper temperature is reached.

Melt butter in a saucepan over low heat. Remove from heat. Blend cocoa into butter with a wooden spoon. Stir in sugar, beaten eggs and water. Add flour and salt; beat well. Add nuts; mix thoroughly.

Into each section of the preheated waffle iron, drop 1 well-rounded teaspoon of batter. Close lid and bake about 1-1/2 minutes. The brownies are done if they do not stick to the top of the waffle iron. Use the tip of a wooden skewer to remove brownies easily. Let cool on racks. Sprinkle with confectioners' sugar, if desired.

No-Bake Cookies

Buckeyes

Leona Carlson

Food Writer (retired), *Rockford Register Star,* Rockford, Illinois

This is one of those recipes that could be called a candy or a cookie. As far as I'm concerned, it's guaranteed to be a winner in any cookie contest and is a sure bet to be the first to disappear in a holiday assortment as well. They freeze well and are handy to have on hand for any special occasion.

Makes 3 to 4 dozen pieces

1 box (16 ounces) confectioners' sugar

1 jar (18 ounces) creamy peanut butter

1/2 cup margarine or butter, softened

1 package (12 ounces) semisweet chocolate morsels

1 (1-inch) square paraffin (optional; see note)

In a large mixing bowl with an electric mixer, combine confectioners' sugar, peanut butter and margarine. Mix well. Roll mixture into bite-size balls. Insert a toothpick in each ball and place on a baking sheet. Freeze for 2 hours.

Before removing balls from freezer, melt chocolate morsels and paraffin in a small saucepan over low heat. Dip frozen balls into chocolate mixture. Place on waxed paper, removing toothpick. These will keep indefinitely in the refrigerator.

Note: The paraffin called for is household paraffin wax, as is used for sealing jelly. The paraffin makes the chocolate easier to handle and shape; it does not affect the taste. Consumption of such a small amount of paraffin is not harmful.

Caramel Chews

Barbara Mihalevich Arciero
Food Writer, *The Times*, Shreveport, Louisiana

I must have been in the third grade when I discovered Caramel Chews. A friend's mother made them for us, and, being an up-and-coming young cook, I asked for the recipe. They're kind of messy to make, but how many 8-year-olds really care about that? For a cool treat on a hot day, stick these in the refrigerator before serving them.

Makes 4 dozen pieces

36 vanilla caramels
3 tablespoons light cream or
　half-and-half
1 cup corn flakes
1 cup crisp rice cereal
　(such as Rice Krispies)

1 cup shredded coconut
1 cup chopped pecans or
　other nuts

Place caramels and cream in top of a double boiler over simmering water. Heat until caramels melt, stirring occasionally.

Toss together corn flakes, rice cereal, coconut and pecans. Add caramel mixture and mix well, using a buttered spoon. Drop by teaspoonfuls onto waxed paper. Let cool.

Caramel Oat Patties

Leni Reed
Free-lance Writer, Reston, Virginia

If you like caramel corn, you'll love these crispy, toffee-like confections made with oat cereal. These cookies make a special after-school or anytime snack. They also can be individually wrapped and tucked into lunch boxes.

Makes 3 dozen cookies

Non-stick cooking spray
6 cups O-shaped toasted
   whole-grain oat cereal
   (such as Cheerios)
1-1/2 cups firmly packed dark
   brown sugar

3/4 cup light corn syrup
1/2 cup water
1-1/2 teaspoons baking soda
Margarine or vegetable oil

Spray a large bowl with non-stick cooking spray. Pour cereal into bowl. Set aside.

In a large saucepan, combine brown sugar, corn syrup and water. Cook over medium heat, stirring occasionally, to hard ball stage (250 degrees on a candy thermometer, or when a hard ball forms upon dropping a small amount of syrup into a cup of cold water). Remove from heat; add baking soda and stir. Mixture will bubble up, so take care that steam from bubbling syrup does not burn hands.

Pour syrup over cereal. Mix well with a spoon that has been greased with margarine or oil. Allow mixture to cool slightly. With hands greased with margarine or oil, form mixture into 2-inch patties. Place patties on a baking sheet that has been sprayed with non-stick cooking spray. Let cool.

When cool, store in an airtight container or wrap individually in plastic wrap.

Chocolate-Caramel Crunches

Rita Barrett

Vice President, International Cookbook Services, White Plains, New York

My aunt used to make these cookies when I was a little girl. I asked her to give me the recipe but, no matter how hard she tried, she couldn't find it anywhere. It wasn't until she moved that it finally appeared, tucked away on a scrap of paper in the back of a very old cookbook. Not only did she give me the recipe, but she also gave me the cookbook. I treasure both.

Makes 25 bars

Crumb Layer:

1/2 cup unsalted butter
1/2 cup granulated sugar
1/4 cup unsweetened
   cocoa powder

2 cups graham cracker
   crumbs
1/3 cup chopped pecans
   or walnuts

Caramel Layer:

1 can (14 ounces) sweetened
   condensed milk
   (not evaporated milk)

3 tablespoons dark corn syrup
2 tablespoons unsalted butter
1 teaspoon vanilla

Topping:

4 squares (1 ounce each)
   semisweet chocolate, melted
   and cooled

For the Crumb Layer: Place butter, sugar and cocoa in a medium saucepan. Cook over low heat, stirring with wooden spoon, until butter is melted and mixture is smooth. Remove from heat; stir in graham cracker crumbs and nuts. Press mixture evenly into a greased 11x7x2-inch baking pan.

For the Caramel Layer: Combine sweetened condensed milk, corn syrup, butter and vanilla in a small saucepan. Cook over moderate heat, stirring, until mixture comes to a rolling boil. Boil 3 minutes, stirring constantly. Pour over crumb layer in pan and spread evenly. Let stand until completely cool.

For Topping: When caramel layer is cool, spread melted chocolate over top. When chocolate is set, run tip of knife around inside edge of pan. Cut into bars and remove from pan.

Chocolate Layer Cookies

Doris Reynolds

Food Columnist, *Naples Daily News,* Naples, Florida

One summer when we were visiting friends in Mass-achuseets, there was a bumper crop of raspberries. We ate raspberries in every conceivable way, but we enjoyed them most when they were simply freshly picked, washed and served with creme fraiche. Because my husband's favorite flavor combination is raspberry and chocolate, my friend, Bella English, and I came up with this sinfully rich cookie that is wonderful all alone, but when served with raspberries or raspberry sherbet, it is absolutely divine.

Makes 30 to 40 bars

1-3/4 cups butter or margarine, divided
1/4 cup granulated sugar
1/3 cup unsweetened cocoa powder
1 teaspoon vanilla
1 egg, lightly beaten
2 cups graham cracker crumbs
1 cup shredded coconut
1/2 cup chopped nuts
6 tablespoons milk
4 tablespoons instant vanilla pudding mix
4 cups sifted confectioners' sugar
8 ounces (1-1/3 cups) semisweet chocolate morsels

In a large saucepan, combine 1/2 cup butter, sugar, cocoa and vanilla. Cook, stirring, over medium heat until well blended. Add egg; cook 5 minutes, stirring constantly. Remove from heat. Blend in graham cracker crumbs, coconut and nuts. Press mixture into a 13x9x2-inch baking pan. Let stand for 15 minutes.

In a large mixing bowl with an electric mixer, beat 1 cup butter until light and fluffy. Combine milk and dry pudding mix; add to butter. Beat well. Gradually add confectioners' sugar, beating until smooth after each addition. Spread over cocoa mixture in pan. Refrigerate 1 hour.

In a small saucepan over low heat, melt chocolate morsels with remaining 1/4 cup butter. Spread over chilled pudding layer. Return to refrigerator and chill thoroughly. To serve, cut into small bars.

Chocolate Ting-a-Lings

Leona Carlson

Food Writer (retired), *Rockford Register Star*, Rockford, Illinois

As a Brownie Girl Scout leader years ago, I divided the troop into groups of three or four and assigned each group a different no-bake cookie to prepare under a mother's supervision. This was one of the recipes. The girls brought all the finished batches to the next troop meeting and packed the assortment in coffee cans, which we had covered with holiday gift wrap. That was their Christmas gift to their parents. This cookie/candy was the most popular of all. They freeze well.

Makes 50 or more treats

2 cups semisweet chocolate morsels

1 cup salted peanuts (whole, not chopped)

2 cups chow mein noodles

Melt chocolate morsels in top of double boiler over hot, but not boiling, water. Remove from heat. Stir in peanuts and crispy noodles. Mix thoroughly. Drop by teaspoonfuls onto foil-lined baking sheets. Refrigerate to harden.

Chocolate Scotcharoos

Barbara Mihalevich Arciero

Food Writer, *The Times*, Shreveport, Louisiana

Norma Rutter, probably the best cook in Marshall, Mo., made Chocolate Scotcharoos for a friend and me when we visited her home years ago. I do not have much patience with drop cookies, so I appreciate this recipe for its simplicity— and its unexpected taste. Scotcharoos are great for potluck dinners, but they can make for messy fingers on hot days.

Makes about 3 dozen cookies

1 cup granulated sugar
1 cup light corn syrup
1 cup peanut butter (smooth or chunky)
6 cups crisp rice cereal (such as Rice Krispies)

1 package (6 ounces) semisweet chocolate morsels
1 package (6 ounces) butterscotch morsels

In a large saucepan, combine sugar and corn syrup; heat until bubbles form around the edge of pan. Remove from heat. Add peanut butter; mix well. Stir in cereal. Press mixture into greased 13x9x2-inch pan.

Melt chocolate morsels and butterscotch morsels in the top of a double boiler or microwave oven; spread over cereal mixture. Let cool, then cut into squares.

Church Windows

Lorrie Guttman
Food Editor, *Tallahassee Democrat*, Tallahassee, Florida

My daughter, Sara, is crazy about marshmallows, so when I asked her to judge a children's recipe contest, she chose marshmallows as the topic. When all was said and done, and we'd eaten what seemed like tons of the sticky stuff at our house, Sara chose these no-bake cookies as the winner. She particularly liked the combination of marshmallows and coconut — and the chocolate made the recipe even richer. As it says in the directions, it's best to serve this in small pieces. It's best, too, to serve it straight from the refrigerator.

Makes about 4 dozen pieces

1/2 cup margarine or butter
1 package (12 ounces) semisweet chocolate morsels
1 bag (10-1/2 ounces) miniature marshmallows (colored ones, if available)

1 bag (7 ounces) shredded coconut

Melt butter in top of double boiler over hot water. Add chocolate morsels; stir until melted, then remove from heat. Let cool. Add marshmallows; stir lightly.

Spread half of the coconut in a greased 9x9x2-inch pan. Spread chocolate mixture over coconut in pan. Top with remaining coconut. Press down with a spoon. Refrigerate until set. When well chilled, cut into small squares.

Date Balls

Lorrie Guttman
Food Editor, *Tallahassee Democrat*, Tallahassee, Florida

Even my children, who don't usually like dates, were wowed by these sweet balls. I chose the recipe as the winner in a "Food Gifts" recipe contest held by our paper. Judy Bledsoe said she has been making these date balls for 25 years. To give them as gifts, she puts the balls in zipper-lock plastic bags, adding extra confectioners' sugar, in case some of the original coating comes off or is absorbed by the cookies. She then puts the bagged cookies in holiday tins.

Makes 3 to 4 dozen balls

7/8 cup (1-3/4 sticks) margarine or butter
1 cup pitted, chopped dates
1 cup granulated sugar

2 cups crisp rice cereal (such as Rice Krispies)
1 cup chopped pecans
Confectioners' sugar

Melt margarine in a heavy saucepan over medium-low heat. Add dates and granulated sugar; cook until thick, stirring often. This should take 5 to 10 minutes. Be sure not to cook the mixture at too high temperature or for too long, or it will become hard.

When mixture is thick, remove from heat; mix in cereal and pecans. Allow to cool about 5 minutes; it should be warm but not hot.

Shape warm mixture into small balls; roll balls in confectioners' sugar.

Instant Chocolate Oatmeal Cookies

Louise F. Dodd
Food Editor, *Courier Herald*, Dublin, Georgia

This is the recipe that all mothers should be able to grab in a hurry when little Susie announces just before bedtime that she has promised to bring cookies for the class party the next morning. Not only is it an unusually delicious cookie, but it is also about the easiest cookie recipe that you can possibly imagine. It might even be good to let little Susie prepare it herself.

Makes 3 to 4 dozen cookies

3 cups quick-cooking rolled oats, uncooked
1 teaspoon vanilla
Dash of salt
1 cup chopped pecans

2 cups granulated sugar
1/2 cup evaporated milk
1/2 cup butter or margarine
2 tablespoons unsweetened cocoa powder

In a large bowl, combine oats, vanilla and salt. Stir in pecans.

In a medium saucepan, combine sugar, evaporated milk, butter and cocoa. Bring to a boil. Remove from heat; stir in oats mixture.

Drop mixture by teaspoonfuls onto waxed paper. Let cool. Store or serve.

Life-Saving Cookies

Louise F. Dodd
Food Editor, *Courier Herald*, Dublin, Georgia

In a terrible panic one busy morning, I suddenly realized that I was supposed to take cookies to garden club. I called my former college roommate and said, "Come up quick with something that I can make in five minutes." She gave me this recipe that her two sons just adore. I soon had it ready and was on my way to the meeting where I discovered, along with my fellow club members, that these are not only quick to prepare, but also delicious.

Makes 3 to 4 dozen cookies

1 cup granulated sugar
1 cup light corn syrup

1 jar (12 ounces) creamy peanut butter
4 cups corn flakes

Combine sugar and corn syrup in a large saucepan and heat just until the sugar is completely dissolved. Stir in peanut butter and corn flakes. Drop by teaspoonfuls onto waxed paper. Let cool completely. Store or serve.

No-Bake Chocolate Oatmeal Cookies

Betty Bernard
Food Editor, *Lake Charles American Press,* Lake Charles, Louisiana

This one really takes "only a minute." When I asked the newsroom staff and several friends and relatives for favorite cookies, I was given this one in about six replies — each calling it a different name. It is certainly popular at my daughter's slumber parties. Unlike fudge, which often doesn't get hard and has to be eaten with a spoon, these cookies are guaranteed to come out just right.

Makes about 3 dozen cookies

2-1/2 cups granulated sugar
2 tablespoons unsweetened
   cocoa powder
1/2 cup margarine or butter
1/2 cup milk

1 teaspoon vanilla
1/2 cup creamy peanut butter
3 cups quick-cooking rolled
   oats, uncooked

In a medium saucepan, combine sugar, cocoa, margarine and milk. Bring to a boil; boil for 1 minute. (Use a timer, and don't overcook!)

Stir in vanilla, peanut butter and oats; mix thoroughly. Drop by spoonfuls onto waxed paper. Let cool.

No-Bake Yummy Bars

Marie D. Galyean
Lifestyle and Food Editor, *Idaho Press-Tribune*, Nampa, Idaho

Food editors are not always the best cooks on a newspaper staff. A "super mom" I worked with on a newspaper certainly had the ability to be food editor, but instead she worked in various jobs, from the education beat and investigative reporting to special projects editor.

But it was her delicious and decorative cakes that were sought after for every party.

She developed and refined these cookie bars from a recipe I published that wasn't half as good. These are rich — almost like candy. They can be made quickly because you can melt the chocolate in the microwave oven while you are cooking the oats mixture on the stove.

Makes 6 to 7 dozen squares

1 cup semisweet chocolate morsels
1 cup butter or margarine (preferably butter)
1/2 cup firmly packed light brown sugar
2 teaspoons vanilla
3 cups quick-cooking rolled oats, uncooked
1/2 cup creamy peanut butter

Melt chocolate morsels in microwave-safe bowl or large measuring cup on High (100 percent) power for 1 minute. Stir and heat another 30 seconds, or until chocolate is melted and smooth. (Or melt chocolate in a small saucepan over low heat on top of the stove.)

Meanwhile, melt butter in large skillet over medium heat. Add brown sugar and vanilla; mix well. Stir in oats. Cook slowly for about 3 minutes.

Put half of the oats mixture in a greased 9x9x2-inch baking pan; press to make an even layer.

Stir peanut butter into melted chocolate. Spread chocolate mixture evenly over oats mixture in pan. Top with remaining half of oats mixture; press gently.

Refrigerate until thoroughly chilled, then cut into 1-inch squares. Serve at room temperature for best flavor.

No-Cook Chocolate-Peanut Butter Yums

Alma Drill

Columnist, Universal Press Syndicate, Bethesda, Maryland

One of the first things most children enjoy in the kitchen is watching cookies being made. It's also the first item most kids want to make themselves. This no-cook chocolate-peanut butter cookie is ideal for a beginning baker. The recipe is an old one that was originally made with creamy peanut butter and fresh peanuts. At some time in its evolution, when I was out of fresh peanuts, the recipe was changed to one made with chunky peanut butter. According to the folks who matter (my family)— "they're better than ever." A warning to those who like peanut butter cups: These cookies are addictive.

Makes about 35 (2-inch) squares or 70 triangles, if squares are cut in half diagonally

3/4 cup firmly packed brown sugar

1 box (16 ounces) confectioners' sugar

1/2 cup plus 1 tablespoon butter, divided

1 jar (28 ounces) chunky peanut butter

1 package (12 ounces) semisweet chocolate morsels

Combine brown sugar, confectioners' sugar, 1/2 cup butter and peanut butter; mix well. Pat mixture into an ungreased 15x10x1-inch jelly-roll pan. Smooth top of mixture.

Melt chocolate morsels and remaining 1 tablespoon butter in top of double boiler or microwave oven. Spread melted chocolate on top of peanut butter mixture.

Refrigerate for 30 minutes to set chocolate. Before cutting into squares or triangles, allow to come to room temperature so chocolate will not crack. Store in refrigerator.

Note: These can be frozen.

Oddballs with Hand-Made Granola

Frances Price
Free-lance Writer, Baltimore, Maryland

To use up an excess of homemade granola, I "invented" this recipe — Oddballs — which is half candy, half health food. I knew food snobs would scorn my recipe if they knew how easy it was to make. But I wanted an unbiased taste test, so I carried a batch down to the haute-est catering joint in town, where the cooks and chefs ate the whole thing and asked for more, never guessing the humble, carefree origins of Oddballs.

Makes about 3 dozen cookies

Oddballs:

4 squares (1 ounce each) semisweet chocolate

12 large marshmallows or 1-1/2 cups miniature marshmallows

1/4 cup butter or margarine

1/2 teaspoon vanilla

3 cups Hand-Made Granola

Hand-Made Granola:

Makes about 12 cups granola

1 box (18 ounces) old-fashioned rolled oats, uncooked

1/2 teaspoon ground cinnamon

1/2 cup shredded coconut (optional)

1/2 cup coarsely chopped nuts — pecans, almonds or walnuts (optional)

1/2 cup wheat germ (optional)

1/4 cup raw sunflower seeds (optional)

2 tablespoons sesame seeds (optional)

1/3 cup neutral-flavored vegetable oil (not olive oil)

1/3 cup honey

1 cup raisins or chopped dried apples, apricots, prunes or figs

For Oddballs: In the top of a double boiler over simmering water, melt chocolate with marshmallows and butter, stirring often, until smooth. Remove from heat. Stir in vanilla, then stir in Hand-Made Granola.

Form mixture into balls the size of walnuts; place balls on waxed paper-lined baking sheets. Refrigerate 30 minutes, or overnight. Store in tightly covered container.

For Hand-Made Granola: In a large mixing bowl, toss oats with cinnamon. Add any or all of these additions: coconut, nuts, wheat germ, sunflower seeds, sesame seeds. Combine oil and honey; pour over oats mixture and mix well with a large spoon.

Spread mixture evenly in a 13x9x2-inch baking pan. Bake in a preheated 350-degree oven 25 to 30 minutes, or until golden brown, turning with a metal spatula every 10 minutes to toast evenly and separate clumps. Let cool to room temperature, then add raisins or dried fruit. Store in tightly covered container.

Orange Sweet Melts

Jeanne Voltz
Cookbook Author, Pittsboro, North Carolina

I took a batch of these to a neighborhood coffee party and the guests inhaled them. Three of the 12 women asked for the recipe and one husband insisted his wife get it. It is my light adaptation of an old favorite, Bourbon Balls, that we made at Christmastime. The elegant flavor and pale blond color makes this new cookie super special.

Makes 24 to 28 cookies

1-1/3 cups fine vanilla wafer crumbs (about 2/3 of a 12-ounce package)
1/2 to 3/4 cup finely chopped pecans, divided
1 cup confectioners' sugar

4 tablespoons partly thawed, undiluted orange juice concentrate
2 tablespoons orange juice
Vegetable oil

To prepare crumbs, place a few vanilla wafers at a time in blender or food processor and run motor in spurts until wafers are in fine crumbs. Place crumbs in a medium mixing bowl. Add 1/2 cup pecans and the confectioners' sugar. Mix well, mashing out any lumps in sugar with a spoon. Slowly stir in orange juice concentrate, then stir in orange juice. Mix thoroughly.

Rub a few drops of vegetable oil onto palms of hands. Pinch off a heaping teaspoonful of dough and, with your hands, roll dough into a ball to shape each cookie. Place balls on waxed paper-lined tray, cover lightly with waxed paper and let dry overnight. If desired, roll cookie balls in remaining 1/4 cup pecans.

Summary Snowballs

Stacy Lam

Reporter, *Macon Telegraph and News*, Macon, Georgia

These no-bake cookies are perfect for summer — you don't have to turn on the oven to make them. The orange and coconut flavor goes well with desserts of fresh fruit at picnics and other summer festivities. They add a bit of extra sweetness for the sweet tooths without being as heavy as some other cookies and candies.

Makes about 4 dozen snowballs

1 box (7-1/2 ounces) vanilla wafers
1-1/4 cups chopped nuts (of your choice)
1/4 cup butter

2/3 cup confectioners' sugar
1/2 cup partly thawed, undiluted orange juice concentrate
2 cups shredded coconut

Crush vanilla wafers. Combine wafer crumbs with nuts in a large mixing bowl; set aside.

In a small saucepan, combine butter, confectioners' sugar and orange juice concentrate. Cook over low heat until butter melts, stirring occasionally. Remove from heat.

Add butter mixture to reserved wafer mixture. Mix by hand until well blended. Roll mixture into 1-inch balls, then roll balls in coconut.

Cookies That Travel Well

Action Vietnam Cookies

Betty Bernard

Food Editor, *Lake Charles American Press,* Lake Charles, Louisiana

These cookies can be frozen or stored in the pantry. They are not fragile and withstand the rigors of shipping. Best of all, they taste good.

Because the cookies get better with age, they were a favorite cookie that an American Press *staff member, Nettie Cardenas, made and shipped to her son assigned to wartime duty in Vietnam. He served two tours of duty — and that's a lot of cookies. So, this recipe makes a large batch.*

Makes 6 dozen cookies

3/4 cup solid vegetable
   shortening
1 cup firmly packed light
   brown sugar
1 egg
1-1/2 cups all-purpose flour
1/2 teaspoon baking soda
1 teaspoon salt
1 teaspoon ground cinnamon
1/4 teaspoon ground nutmeg
1/2 cup coarsely chopped
   walnuts

1/2 cup semisweet chocolate
   morsels
   (plain or mint flavored)
1/2 cup shredded coconut
1/2 cup raisins dredged in 1
   tablespoon all-purpose flour
1 cup mashed ripe
   bananas (2 or 3)
1-3/4 cups quick-cooking rolled
   oats, uncooked

In a large mixing bowl with an electric mixer, beat together shortening and brown sugar. Add egg and continue beating until ingredients are well blended.

Sift together flour, baking soda, salt, cinnamon and nutmeg. Add flour mixture to shortening mixture, stirring to keep batter well blended. Add walnuts, chocolate morsels, coconut, raisins and bananas; mix well. Gradually stir in oats, mixing well.

Drop dough from end of teaspoon onto lightly greased baking sheets. Bake in a preheated 375-degree oven 12 minutes, or until done.

Tip: To save time spent baking, drop batter on cookie sheet lined with heavy-duty aluminum foil. When done and slightly cooled, cookies will "peel" off the foil. Liner can be used again, or having two or three foil liners ready with cookie batches for baking will hasten the baking episode considerably.

Apple Oatmeal Squares

Leni Reed
Free-lance Writer, Reston, Virginia

These great-tasting cookies are perfect for packing into lunch boxes. The applesauce keeps them soft and moist and they travel well. They make a tasty treat for lunch or breakfast-on-the-run. You might want to make a double batch, but be sure to bake them in two separate pans.

Makes 24 squares

1 cup margarine, softened
1 cup firmly packed dark brown sugar
1 cup chunky applesauce (with no sugar added)
1 teaspoon vanilla

4 cups quick-cooking rolled oats, uncooked
1/2 cup chopped pecans
1 tablespoon ground cinnamon
1 teaspoon baking powder

In a medium mixing bowl, combine margarine, brown sugar, applesauce and vanilla. Stir by hand until well blended. Add oats, pecans, cinnamon and baking powder; mix well.

Spray a 13x9x2-inch baking pan with non-stick cooking spray. Press mixture into prepared pan. It is helpful to wet hands before pressing mixture into pan.

Bake in a preheated 325-degree oven 30 minutes, or until edges are golden brown. Let cool thoroughly. Cut into squares. Store in an airtight container.

Apricot Dream Chews

Mary Denise Scourtes

Food Writer, *The Tampa Tribune*, Tampa, Florida

The combination of apricots and oats is a prize-winning one in these easy bar cookies. This combination is a childhood favorite that was packed with fried chicken and potato salad for every trip to the beach. These cookies keep well for days, so there is no need to freeze them; however, they do freeze well.

Makes 3 dozen cookies

Filling:

1-1/2 cups dried apricots

1-1/2 cups water

1/4 cup honey

Base:

1-1/3 cups firmly packed
   brown sugar

1 cup butter, softened

1-1/2 cups quick-cooking or
   old-fashioned rolled oats,
   uncooked

1-1/2 cups all-purpose flour

1/2 teaspoon baking soda

1/2 teaspoon salt

1/2 cup chopped pecans

Confectioners' sugar (optional)

Combine apricots and water in a medium saucepan. Simmer, uncovered, over medium heat for 15 minutes. Drain; let cool, then chop. Stir honey into chopped apricots.

In large bowl, beat brown sugar and butter until fluffy (by hand or with a hand-held electric mixer). Add oats, flour, baking soda and salt; beat until well mixed. Stir in pecans.

Measure 2 cups oats mixture and reserve for topping. Press remaining oats mixture in bottom of an ungreased 13x9x2-inch baking pan. Bake in a preheated 375-degree oven 10 minutes, or until crust is light brown.

Spread apricot filling evenly over crust to within 1/2-inch of sides of pan. Sprinkle reserved 2 cups oats mixture over apricot filling. Return to 375-degree oven and bake 25 minutes, or until golden. Let cool in pan. Cut into squares. Dust with confectioners' sugar, if desired.

Carrot Bars

Marie D. Galyean

Lifestyle and Food Editor, *Idaho Press-Tribune*, Nampa, Idaho

This carrot bar recipe is from my mother, Margaret Groat Devine. Because she was born before the turn of the century and grew up in the early 1900s, I suspect it originally called for grated or chopped carrots, instead of baby food.

However, Mama was a lady who knew how to improve things and save time. She was widowed in 1941 and had to work to support her family.

This quick recipe was one of her favorites. Her recipe called for dark raisins, but I like the way the golden raisins blend in with the golden color of the bars. Use whichever you prefer — or have handy. I also have discovered that these cookies pack well for lunch boxes.

Makes 3 dozen bars

1 cup golden raisins
4 eggs, beaten
1-1/4 cups vegetable oil
3 jars (4 ounces each) strained carrots (baby food)
1 teaspoon vanilla
1-1/2 cups granulated sugar

2-1/2 cups all-purpose flour
2 teaspoons baking soda
1 teaspoon salt
1 teaspoon ground cinnamon
1/4 teaspoon ground cloves
1/4 teaspoon ground cardamom
1/4 teaspoon ground nutmeg

Cover raisins with hot water; let soak (plump) while you assemble other ingredients. Drain well.

In a large bowl, combine eggs, oil, carrots, vanilla, sugar, flour, baking soda, salt, cinnamon, cloves, cardamom and nutmeg. Mix well. Stir in drained raisins.

Pour batter into a greased 15x10x1-inch jelly-roll pan. Bake in a preheated 350-degree oven 25 minutes, or until done. Let cool in pan. Cut into bars.

Note: These carrot bars make an elegant dessert when topped with a dollop of whipped cream.

Chocolate Chip Brownies

Sally Cappon

Food Writer, *Santa Barbara News-Press*, Santa Barbara, California

Years ago, when I attended journalism school at the University of Wisconsin, all my friends' mothers sent boxes brimming with wonderful home-baked goodies. My mother worked outside the home, and she didn't have time to spend hours in the kitchen. She made and sent one thing: chocolate chip brownies. Using just three "convenience" ingredients plus confectioners' sugar, these easy-to-pack bar cookies were so good that my roommates lay in wait for her packages and ripped them open before I got home from class. If there was a crumb left, I was lucky. They taste just as good today.

Makes 36 small brownies

1 package (6 ounces) semisweet chocolate morsels
21 graham cracker squares, crushed

1 can (14 ounces) sweetened condensed milk (not evaporated milk)
Confectioners' sugar

Grease an 8x8x2-inch baking pan; line pan with waxed paper and grease again.

In a mixing bowl, combine chocolate morsels, crushed graham crackers and sweetened condensed milk. Press mixture into prepared pan.

Bake in a preheated 375-degree oven 30 minutes. Turn out of pan and peel off waxed paper while still warm. Cut into squares. Roll squares in confectioners' sugar.

Chocolate Fudge Brownies

Beth Winsten Orenstein
Staff Writer, *The Express*, Easton, Pennsylvania

I'm not sure if these brownies are fudge or cookies, they're so rich. The recipe has been in my husband's family for years. His mother used to make him a batch and mail them to him at college. He was always the most popular man in the dorm the day they arrived. I know they're responsible for at least a few of the pounds I've put on since meeting him. We like to make them whenever we're asked to bring a dessert to a dinner or party because there isn't anyone who doesn't like them. They keep well in the refrigerator — if they last that long, that is.

Makes 16 brownies

4 squares (1 ounce each) unsweetened chocolate
1 cup butter
2 eggs

2 cups granulated sugar
1 cup all-purpose flour
2 teaspoons vanilla
Dash salt

In a medium saucepan over low heat, melt chocolate and butter. Stir to mix.

Break eggs into a mixing bowl, but do not beat. Add sugar, flour, vanilla and salt to eggs; mix well. Stir in chocolate mixture.

Pour batter into an ungreased 8x8x2-inch baking pan. Bake in a preheated 350-degree oven 35 to 40 minutes, or until toothpick comes out dry. Do not overcook. Let brownies cool in pan before cutting into squares.

Chocolate Scotch Shortbread

Frances Price
Food Columnist, Baltimore, Maryland

For traditional buttery, crumbly Scotch Shortbread, just omit the chocolate in this recipe. Either version is wonderful with tea or coffee in the late afternoon, with a glass of milk late at night, for lunch box treats, or for pairing with fresh fruit desserts such as peaches or strawberries.

Makes 25 squares

2 squares (1 ounce each) semisweet chocolate
3/4 cup butter, at room temperature

1/2 cup firmly packed light brown sugar
1-1/2 cups all-purpose flour

Melt chocolate in the top of a double boiler over hot water or in microwave oven; set aside.

In a large mixing bowl with an electric mixer on medium speed, beat butter until fluffy. Add brown sugar; beat until very light and fluffy. Reduce mixer speed to low, blend in melted chocolate, then flour.

Spread dough evenly in ungreased 8x8x2-inch baking pan. Prick surface with fork tines. Bake in a preheated 350-degree oven 20 to 25 minutes, or until wooden pick inserted in center comes out clean. Let cool in pan on rack 10 to 15 minutes, then cut into squares.

Crispy Oat Treats

Toni Burks

Food Editor, *Roanoke Times & World-News,* Roanoke, Virginia

"You must try this!" an aunt wrote on the recipe card when she shared this cookie. She obtained the recipe from a friend who got it from a friend — and isn't that the way good things are perpetuated? It's a cookie jar favorite that is ideal for lunch boxes and after-school snacking. Because it freezes so well, it's handy to have around.

Makes about 10 dozen

1 cup margarine or butter, softened (if margarine is used, use regular margarine, not low-calorie or whipped margarine)
1 cup granulated sugar
1 cup firmly packed light or dark brown sugar
1 egg
1 cup vegetable oil
1 teaspoon vanilla
3-1/2 cups all-purpose flour
1 teaspoon baking soda
1/2 teaspoon salt
1 cup old-fashioned rolled oats, uncooked
1 cup granola-type cereal
1 cup shredded coconut
1/2 cup chopped pecans or walnuts

In a large bowl with an electric mixer on medium speed, beat margarine until light and fluffy. Gradually add granulated sugar and brown sugar, beating well. Add egg; beat well. Add oil and vanilla; mix well. Combine flour, baking soda and salt; add to margarine mixture and blend well. Stir in oats, cereal, coconut and nuts.

Shape dough into 1-inch balls; place balls on ungreased baking sheet. Flatten each ball of dough with tines of a fork. Bake in a preheated 325-degree oven 15 minutes. Let cool slightly, then transfer cookies to wire rack to cool completely.

Ginger Cookies

Stacy Lam

Reporter, *Macon Telegraph and News,* Macon, Georgia

Ginger cookies were popular when my father was growing up during the 1930s in rural Virginia because they don't require granulated sugar, which was difficult to come by back then.

These cookies travel well. I always loved getting them in a "care" package from home during my college days, but they didn't last long once my roommates discovered them.

They're also good for any occasion — a luncheon, afternoon tea or after-dinner coffee — when made as a drop cookie. Or the dough can be rolled out on waxed paper and cut into gingerbread men as a special treat for children.

Makes about 4 dozen cookies

3/4 cup solid vegetable shortening
1 cup firmly packed dark brown sugar
1 egg
1/4 cup molasses

2-1/4 cups all-purpose flour
2 teaspoons baking soda
1/2 teaspoon ground cloves
1 teaspoon ground cinnamon
2 teaspoons ground ginger

In a large mixing bowl, combine by hand the shortening, brown sugar, egg, molasses, flour, baking soda, cloves, cinnamon and ginger; mix well. Roll dough into balls, using 1 teaspoon dough for each ball. Place balls on greased baking sheet. Press flat with the bottom of a glass.

Bake in a preheated 375-degree oven 8 minutes, or until done. Let cookies cool before removing from baking sheet.

Note: The dough can be rolled out on waxed paper and cut out with cookie cutters, if desired.

Hazelnut-Chocolate Cookies

Barbara Bloch
President, International Cookbook Services, White Plains, New York

*No visit to camp was ever complete without a big box
of these cookies for my children and their bunk mates—
and an extra box for the counselors. The cookies were
always at the top of a long list of "please bring."*

Makes 3 dozen cookies

3/4 cup firmly packed brown
  sugar
1/2 cup unsalted butter, softened
2 tablespoons molasses
1 egg
2 cups all-purpose flour
1 teaspoon baking powder

1 teaspoon ground cinnamon
1/2 cup finely chopped
  hazelnuts (filberts) or
  almonds
2 squares (1 ounce each)
  semisweet chocolate,
  chopped

In a medium bowl with an electric mixer on medium speed, beat brown sugar and butter until light and fluffy. Add molasses and egg; beat until blended. Sift flour, baking powder and cinnamon over butter mixture. Mix with a wooden spoon. Add hazelnuts and chocolate; stir until blended.

Shape dough into a log, about 2 inches thick. Wrap log in waxed paper and refrigerate 3 hours, or until firm.

Cut dough into 1/4-inch thick slices. Place slices, about 1 inch apart, on greased baking sheets.

Bake in a preheated 375-degree oven 10 to 12 minutes, or until edges are lightly browned. Remove from baking sheets and let cool completely on wire racks.

Honey Almond Crunch

Marlene Sorosky
Free-lance Writer, Hunt Valley, Maryland

For more than 20 years, I have taught holiday classes on gifts to make from your kitchen. One of the most requested and popular recipes from these classes is this rich, crisp confection that is round like a cookie and crunchy and buttery like toffee. You can vary the size by baking the batter in aluminum pie pans or individual muffin cups. These travel well and will keep in the refrigerator indefinitely — if you hide them.

Makes 29 (2-inch) or 5 (8-inch) cookies

1 cup unsalted butter
1 cup granulated sugar
1/3 cup honey
1/3 cup heavy cream
1/4 teaspoon almond extract

1 pound sliced almonds
8 squares (1 ounce each) semisweet chocolate, melted (optional)

Butter 5 (8-inch) aluminum pie pans or 29 (2-inch) muffin cups or tartlet pans. Set aside.

In a medium saucepan with a heavy bottom, combine butter, sugar, honey, cream and almond extract. Bring to a boil over moderate heat, stirring frequently. When mixture comes to a boil, cook, stirring constantly, for 1-1/2 minutes. Remove from heat and stir in almonds.

Divide mixture among prepared pans, using a rounded soup spoon to fill muffin cups. Pat mixture evenly in bottom of pans using spoon or fingers dipped in cold water. Pans should be filled about 1/2-inch deep.

Bake in a preheated 375-degree oven 8 to 12 minutes, or until golden brown. Timing will depend on type of pan used. Remove pans from oven and let cool slightly.

Refrigerate 5 to 10 minutes, or until just firm enough to go around edges with tip of a sharp knife. Remove from pans to waxed paper. Let cool completely.

If desired, spread or drizzle melted chocolate on flat side. Refrigerate until chocolate is hardened.

Note: These cookies can be stored in a cool place in an airtight container up to one month, or refrigerated indefinitely.

Muesli Bars

Rita Barrett
Vice President, International Cookbook Services, White Plains, New York

These bars are a popular lunch box treat in our family because they taste so good. Hazelnuts, coconut and sesame seeds make an unusual flavor combination.

Makes 20 bars

1/2 cup unsalted butter, softened
1/3 cup firmly packed brown sugar
3 tablespoons honey
1 cup quick-cooking rolled oats, uncooked

1/3 cup chopped hazelnuts (filberts), almonds or macadamia nuts
1/3 cup shredded coconut
1/3 cup sesame seeds

In a medium saucepan over low heat, combine butter, brown sugar and honey. Cook, stirring, until butter is melted and sugar is dissolved. Remove from heat. Add oats, hazelnuts, coconut and sesame seeds. Mix with a wooden spoon until well combined. Press mixture evenly into greased 11x7x2-inch baking pan.

Bake in a preheated 350-degree oven 15 to 18 minutes, or until top is golden brown. Let cool in pan on wire rack 10 minutes. Score into bars, then let cool completely in pan on rack. Cut into bars and remove from pan.

Variation: Dip bars halfway into melted chocolate. Place on wire racks until chocolate is set.

Oat Bran-Carrot Brownies

Rita Barrett
Vice President, International Cookbook Services, White Plains, New York

*When my daughter, Sara, was in sixth grade, she was
given an assignment for health class that required her
to bring a healthful snack to school. She was deter-
mined to create an original snack, so we went to work
in the kitchen and developed the following recipe. Her
classmates loved the cookies and no one realized they
had eaten a healthful vegetable and oat bran flakes until
Sara read the recipe to the class.*

Makes 3 dozen brownies

1 box (21 ounces) brownie mix
1 cup oat bran flakes
1 cup grated carrots
2 eggs

1/2 cup water
1/4 cup sunflower or
  vegetable oil
1 teaspoon ground cinnamon

Place dry brownie mix in a large bowl. Add oat bran, carrots, eggs, water, oil and cinnamon; mix with wooden spoon until well blended. Spread mixture evenly in greased 13x9x2-inch baking pan.

Bake in a preheated 350-degree oven 30 minutes. Let cool completely in pan on wire rack. When cool, cut into 1-1/2 x 2-1/8-inch bars and remove from pan.

Praline Cookies

Frances Price
Food Columnist, Baltimore, Maryland

Last fall, I was startled to hear Candice Bergen and Colleen Dewhurst, playing Murphy Brown and her mother on the hit TV show, reminiscing about praline cookies. I, too, have fond memories of praline cookies made by my Aunt Leenie, more formally known as Aileen. Here is her recipe, which I believed for years to be the only one in existence. With a taste similar to the New Orleans confection of the same name, Leenie's Praline Cookies are easily made with the same ingredients of brown sugar, pecans and butter. These travel well and make good gifts for friends far away.

Makes about 3 dozen cookies

1/2 cup butter
1 cup firmly packed dark or light brown sugar
1 egg, lightly beaten
1-1/4 cups sifted all-purpose flour

1 teaspoon vanilla
1 cup pecan pieces (or other nuts)

In a 2-quart saucepan, melt butter over low heat. Remove from heat; stir in brown sugar until blended. Beat in egg, then flour, vanilla and pecans.

Drop dough by rounded teaspoonfuls, 2 inches apart, onto ungreased baking sheets. Bake in a preheated 375-degree oven 8 to 10 minutes, or until lightly browned and crisp. Remove immediately from baking sheet and let cool on racks or waxed paper.

Pfeffernüesse

Frances Price
Food Columnist, Baltimore, Maryland

The recipe for these spicy cookies was given to me long ago by a homesick German bride. It makes a huge batch, enough for gift-giving with plenty left for your family. Pfeffernüesse are sturdy travelers, nice for mailing to faraway friends. Don't despair over the length of the ingredient list; the seven spices make it seem longer than it really is.

Makes about 7 dozen cookies

8 ounces candied citron
4 ounces candied orange peel
4 cups sifted all-purpose flour
1 tablespoon ground cinnamon
1 tablespoon ground cardamom
1 teaspoon ground cloves
1 teaspoon ground nutmeg
1 teaspoon baking soda
1/2 teaspoon ground black pepper
1 teaspoon anise seeds

5 eggs, separated
2 tablespoons butter, at room temperature
1-1/2 teaspoons grated lemon peel
2-1/2 cups granulated sugar
1-1/2 cups confectioners' sugar
2 to 3 tablespoons milk
Additional confectioners' sugar (optional)

Coarsely grind the citron and orange peel with grinder fitted with coarse blade; set aside.

Sift flour with cinnamon, cardamom, cloves, nutmeg, baking soda and pepper. Sprinkle anise seeds over flour mixture. Set aside.

In a large mixing bowl with an electric mixer on medium speed, beat egg yolks with butter and lemon peel until smooth. Reduce speed to low and beat in granulated sugar. Set aside.

Beat egg whites in clean mixer bowl with an electric mixer or by hand until stiff peaks form. On low speed of an electric mixer, gently fold reserved egg yolk mixture into beaten egg whites. Blend in reserved flour mixture, using your hands. Blend in reserved coarsely ground candied citron and orange peel.

Shape dough into balls the size of a small walnut; place balls, 1 inch apart, on ungreased baking sheets. Let stand, uncovered, 8 hours, or overnight.

Bake in a preheated 350-degree oven 15 minutes, or until double in size and lightly browned. Remove from baking sheets and let cool to room temperature.

Mix confectioners' sugar with enough milk to form a thin glaze; drizzle glaze over cookies. If desired, after glaze has hardened, shake cookies gently in paper bag containing additional confectioners' sugar.

Raisin Nut Bars

Muriel Stevens
Food Editor, *Las Vegas Sun*, Las Vegas, Nevada

This tasty cookie is quickly made. It's the perfect lunch box extra for kids. Tell them it's a new version of a carrot stick and see how they respond.

Makes 12 dozen small cookies

2 cups all-purpose flour
1 teaspoon baking powder
1/4 teaspoon baking soda
1/4 teaspoon salt
1 teaspoon ground cinnamon
1/2 teaspoon ground nutmeg
2 cups lightly crushed corn flakes, or similar cereal
1/2 cup butter or margarine

1/2 cup granulated sugar
1/2 cup firmly packed light brown sugar
2 eggs
1 cup finely shredded carrots
1 cup raisins
1 cup coarsely chopped nuts
1/3 cup milk

Sift flour; measure 2 cups. Sift flour again along with baking powder, baking soda, salt, cinnamon and nutmeg. Stir in corn flakes.

In a large mixing bowl with an electric mixer, beat butter, granulated sugar and brown sugar until fluffy. Add eggs; beat thoroughly. Stir in carrots, raisins, nuts and milk. Add flour mixture; stir until well blended.

Drop dough by teaspoonfuls, 2 inches apart, onto lightly greased baking sheets. Bake in a preheated 375-degree oven 12 minutes, or until lightly browned.

Note: Cookies are crunchy when they're fresh from the oven. They soften if kept more than a day.

Walnut Bars

Jeanne Voltz
Cookbook Author, Pittsboro, North Carolina

Our house in Encino, California, sat amid eight walnut trees, leftovers from the land's previous use as a commercial walnut grove. Being amateur tree growers, our yield was hardly worth the effort. But with careful picking over of nuts, we salvaged enough to bake a few batches of these chewy cookies each year. This cookie is rugged, so it's good to tote on picnics. I like these cookies with fresh berries or peaches.

Makes 2-1/2 dozen bars

3 egg whites
1 teaspoon lemon juice
1 cup firmly packed dark brown sugar
1 cup all-purpose or unbleached flour

1/2 teaspoon baking powder
1/8 teaspoon salt
1 teaspoon vanilla
1-1/2 to 2 cups coarsely chopped walnuts

In a medium bowl with an electric mixer, beat egg whites until foamy throughout. Add lemon juice; beat until stiff. Beat in brown sugar, a few tablespoons at a time. Gradually beat in flour, baking powder, salt and vanilla. Fold in walnuts.

Spread dough in a greased 8x8x2-inch baking pan. Bake in a preheated 300-degree oven 1 hour, or until pick inserted in center comes out clean. Let cool in pan 10 to 15 minutes. Cut into bars.

Bar Cookies

Almond Bars

Rita Barrett
Vice President, International Cookbook Services, White Plains, New York

*These chewy cookies are almost like thin cakes. They
are so easy to make that I taught my daughters how to
make them when they were just learning how to cook.
Now they make them whenever they discover we have no
cookies in the pantry.*

Makes 18 bars

1 cup granulated sugar
3 eggs
1 can (12 ounces) almond
   filling

3/4 cup all-purpose flour
1 teaspoon baking powder
18 whole blanched almonds

In a medium mixing bowl with an electric mixer on medium speed, beat sugar and eggs until thick and foamy. Add almond filling; beat until well blended. Combine flour and baking powder; fold into almond mixture.

Spread batter evenly in greased 13x9x2-inch baking pan. Press almonds gently on top of batter in even rows (6 rows across length of pan and 3 rows across width of pan).

Bake in a preheated 350-degree oven 40 to 45 minutes, or until toothpick inserted into center comes out clean. Let cool completely in pan on a wire rack. Cut into bars and remove from pan.

Angel Squares

Mary Denise Scourtes
Food Writer, *The Tampa Tribune*, Tampa, Florida

Angel Squares are the easiest and quickest of all cookies to produce. Because they are a cross between a cookie and a candy, it's best to have a little whipped cream around to cover any crumbly bars. After you take one bite, you'll be hooked. Best of all, no one can ever guess that chocolate sandwich cookies are the base.

Makes 2 dozen cookies

6 egg whites
1/4 teaspoon salt
2 teaspoons baking powder
1-1/3 cups granulated sugar

20 cream-filled chocolate sandwich cookies (such as Oreo or Hydrox), crushed
1 cup chopped pecans
Whipped cream, for garnish

In a mixing bowl with an electric mixer, beat egg whites until stiff. Beat in salt, baking powder and sugar. Fold in crushed cookies and pecans. Pour into a greased 13x9x2-inch baking pan. Bake in a preheated 350-degree oven 35 to 40 minutes.

Cut into squares. Garnish with whipped cream to hide any crumbly cuts.

Butter Bars

Beth Winsten Orenstein
Staff Writer, *The Express*, Easton, Pennsylvania

My mother-in-law, Helen Orenstein, recommends these butter cookies because the recipe never fails. Also, there's no waste. The egg yolk is used in the batter while the egg white is brushed on top. Anyone who bakes is likely to have all the ingredients on hand. The cookies taste different when topped with sprinkles or ground nuts.

Makes 3 to 4 dozen bars

1 cup butter
3/4 cup granulated sugar
1 egg, separated
2 cups all-purpose flour

1 teaspoon vanilla
1/2 teaspoon almond extract
Candy sprinkles or ground nuts
  (optional)

In a large bowl with an electric mixer, beat butter and sugar until fluffy. Beat in egg yolk, flour, vanilla and almond extract. Spread dough in a 15x10x1-inch jelly-roll pan. Brush the top of the dough with unbeaten egg white. If desired, scatter sprinkles or nuts on top.

Bake in a preheated 325-degree oven 30 minutes, or until done. Let cool in pan, then cut into bars.

Chewy Cream Cheese Squares

Carolyn Flournoy
Cooking Columnist, *The Times*, Shreveport, Louisiana

One of my daughters-in-law is business editor of a major Louisiana newspaper, but she still finds time to make some delectable dishes. She gave me this recipe, which she obtained from a male co-worker. Now I serve it at all family get-togethers.

Makes 16 squares

1/2 cup firmly packed dark
  brown sugar
1/4 cup unsalted butter
1 cup buttermilk baking mix
2/3 cup chopped pecans
1 package (8 ounces) cream
  cheese, softened

1/4 cup granulated sugar
1 tablespoon lemon juice
2-1/2 teaspoons milk
1/2 teaspoon vanilla
1 egg

In a mixing bowl with an electric mixer, beat brown sugar and butter until fluffy. Stir in baking mix and pecans until mixture is crumbly. Measure 1 cup brown sugar mixture and set aside for topping. Press remaining brown sugar mixture into a greased 8x8x2-inch baking pan, covering entire bottom. Bake in a preheated 350-degree oven 12 minutes.

Meanwhile, in another mixing bowl, combine cream cheese and granulated sugar until blended. Beat in lemon juice, milk, vanilla and egg until smooth.

Spread cream cheese mixture over baked layer in pan; sprinkle reserved 1 cup brown sugar mixture over top. Return to 350-degree oven and bake about 25 minutes, or until center is firm. Allow to cool before cutting into 2-inch squares. Store cookies in refrigerator.

Chocolate Carrot Brownies

Doris Reynolds

Food Columnist, *Naples Daily News*, Naples, Florida

My family used to spend several months each year in the mountains of North Carolina. We often drove to Asheville to pick up baked goods at a bakery called The Dough Boys. They've been out of business for many years, but I still have their recipe for Chocolate Carrot Brownies. For a long time they refused to part with the recipe, but one Christmas I got a card from the two men who had owned the bakery telling me they were opening a restaurant in Michigan. As their Christmas present to me they gave me their precious recipe. I've published it in my column and often bake it for friends who need a lift. It's almost as effective as chicken soup.

Makes 16 brownies

8 ounces bittersweet chocolate
1/2 cup unsalted butter
3/4 cup all-purpose flour
1/2 cup granulated sugar
1 teaspoon salt
3 eggs
1 cup finely shredded carrots
  (about 3 medium carrots)

3/4 cup chopped pecans or
  walnuts
Grated zest of 1 orange
1 teaspoon vanilla
1/3 cup dark or golden raisins
  (optional)

Line an 8x8x2-inch baking pan with aluminum foil, then butter lightly; set aside.

Melt chocolate and butter in top of a double boiler over simmering water. Stir to blend, then remove from heat and set aside.

Sift flour, sugar and salt into a large bowl.

With a wooden spoon, beat eggs into reserved chocolate mixture, one egg at a time. Pour chocolate mixture into the flour mixture; blend well. Stir in carrots, nuts, orange zest, vanilla and raisins.

Pour batter into prepared baking pan. Bake in the middle of a preheated 350-degree oven about 30 minutes, or until a knife or toothpick inserted in the center comes out clean. Remove the pan from the oven and let brownies cool in pan on a wire rack. Cut into squares.

Chocolate Hazelnut Brownies

Lori Longbotham
Food Columnist, *New York Post*, New York, New York

*These are rich, delicious, sophisticated brownies —
with great appeal for grown-ups. They have a terrific,
intense, chocolate flavor. The sweetness of hazelnuts
really rounds out the flavor. These brownies would be
a great dessert for a picnic or even a fancy dinner party
— serving them with vanilla ice cream would be ideal.*

Makes 16 brownies

12 ounces bittersweet or semisweet (not unsweetened) chocolate, coarsely chopped, divided
3/4 cup unsalted butter
1/4 cup hazelnut oil or vegetable oil

1-1/2 cups granulated sugar
4 eggs
1 teaspoon vanilla
1 cup all-purpose flour, sifted
3/4 cup hazelnuts (filberts), toasted, skinned and coarsely chopped

Combine 4 ounces chocolate, butter and oil in the top of a double boiler over simmering water. Heat until chocolate and butter melt, stirring occasionally. Let cool.

Beat sugar, eggs and vanilla in a mixing bowl until mixed. Add melted chocolate mixture and flour; stir until blended. Stir in the remaining 8 ounces chocolate and hazelnuts.

Pour batter into buttered 9x9x2-inch baking pan. Bake in a pre-heated 350-degree oven about 55 minutes, or until a toothpick inserted in center comes out sticky but not wet. Let cool completely, then cut into squares.

Coconut Island Squares

Paula M. Galusha

Food Writer, *Oklahoma Home & Lifestyle Magazine*, Tulsa, Oklahoma

After attending a convention in Hawaii, I was inspired to develop a recipe to commemorate our glorious trip. Now, when I prepare these cookies, I can remember the beautiful beaches, the gorgeous sunsets and the abundance of fresh fish and fruit.

Makes 3 dozen squares

1/2 cup butter or margarine
1/4 cup granulated sugar
1 cup plus 2 tablespoons all-purpose flour, divided
3/4 cup quick-cooking rolled oats, uncooked
1/4 teaspoon salt
1/4 teaspoon baking soda

2 eggs
3/4 cup firmly packed brown sugar
1/2 teaspoon ground cinnamon
1/2 teaspoon almond extract
1/2 cup chopped nuts
3/4 cup shredded coconut

In a small mixing bowl with an electric mixer on medium speed, beat butter and sugar for 1 minute. Add 1 cup flour, oats, salt and baking soda. Beat on low speed just until blended.

Press dough into bottom of a greased 9x9x2-inch baking pan. Bake in a preheated 350-degree oven 10 to 12 minutes, or until lightly browned.

In a small mixing bowl with an electric mixer, beat eggs until light. Gradually add brown sugar, beating just until blended. Add remaining 2 tablespoons flour, cinnamon and almond extract. Mix well. Stir in nuts.

Spread nut mixture over partly baked dough. Sprinkle with coconut. Return to 350-degree oven and bake 20 minutes. Let cool in pan on rack. Cut into squares.

Coconut Triangles

Rita Barrett
Vice President, International Cookbook Services, White Plains, New York

*These delicious Coconut Triangles add good variety
to a tray of assorted cookies. The shape and texture of
the cookie differ from most other cookies, making them
a welcome addition when several people bring cookies
to a cooperative event. These cookies sell quickly at
bake sales.*

Makes 3 dozen triangles

1 cup granulated sugar, divided
2/3 cup unsalted butter, softened, divided
1 egg
1 teaspoon vanilla
1-1/4 cups all-purpose flour
1/2 teaspoon baking powder
1/4 cup apricot jam
2 tablespoons water
1-1/2 cups shredded coconut
2 squares (1 ounce each) semisweet chocolate, melted

In a large mixing bowl with an electric mixer on medium speed, beat 1/2 cup sugar, 1/3 cup butter, egg and vanilla until light and fluffy. Combine flour and baking powder; add to sugar mixture. Mix well. Spread or pat dough evenly into greased 13x9x2-inch baking pan. Spread jam over dough.

Melt remaining 1/3 cup butter in a small saucepan. Add remaining 1/2 cup sugar and water. Heat and stir until blended. Remove from heat and stir in coconut. Spoon coconut mixture evenly over jam.

Bake in a preheated 350-degree oven 25 to 30 minutes, or until top is golden brown. Let cool in pan on wire rack 15 minutes. While still warm, cut into bars. Cut each bar in half diagonally to make triangles. Remove from pan and let cool completely on wire racks.

Dip 2 opposite points of each triangle into melted chocolate. Let stand on wire racks until chocolate is set.

Date Oatmeal Bars

Kathleen Stang
Free-lance Food Writer, Seattle, Washington

My mother-in-law, Mildred Stang, used to live in Palm Desert, California, where fresh dates are plentiful. For this recipe, she prefers the Deglet Noor variety — the kind sold in most grocery stores. Her date oatmeal cookies are rich and wonderful. She still makes them for us "kids" at Christmas time.

Makes 2 dozen cookies

2 cups pitted, chopped dates
1 tablespoon plus 1 cup all-purpose flour, divided
1 cup water
1 teaspoon vanilla
1 teaspoon baking soda

1 cup firmly packed brown sugar
2 cups quick-cooking rolled oats, uncooked
1/2 cup butter or margarine, softened

Toss dates with 1 tablespoon flour in saucepan. Stir in water. Simmer 10 minutes, or until thickened. Remove from heat. Stir in vanilla. Let cool.

Combine remaining 1 cup flour, baking soda, brown sugar and oats. Add butter; mix well.

Spray a 13x9x2-inch baking pan with non-stick spray. Pat half of oats mixture into pan. Spread date mixture on top. Sprinkle remaining oats mixture over date mixture. Firm by patting with hand.

Bake in a preheated 375-degree oven about 20 minutes, or until done. Let cool in pan on a wire rack. Cut into squares.

Easy Praline Squares

Beth Whitley Duke
Food Editor, *Amarillo Globe-News*, Amarillo, Texas

Pralines are a traditional Mexican sweet served to take the fire out of a hot Tex-Mex meal. These easy squares use graham crackers as a base for a praline taste without having to make the actual brown sugar candy.

Makes about 2 dozen cookies

Graham crackers
1 cup firmly packed brown
   sugar

10 tablespoons margarine
1/4 teaspoon cream of tartar
1 cup finely chopped pecans

Break enough graham crackers into individual rectangles to cover the bottom of a 15x10x1-inch jelly-roll pan.

In a saucepan or microwave-safe mixing bowl, bring brown sugar and margarine to a boil. (If using a microwave oven, watch the mixture carefully.)

Add cream of tartar and pecans to boiling brown sugar mixture. Pour over graham crackers. Bake in a preheated 325-degree oven 10 minutes. Remove from pan while still warm and separate into squares.

Fruit and Nut Surprise Bars

Barbara Bloch

President, International Cookbook Services, White Plains, New York

The thing I like so much about these cookies is that I can use any kind of dried fruit and any kind of chopped nuts in any combination I want. As a result, these cookies are different every time I make them. Sometimes I even use more than one kind of fruit. It's a recipe that permits you to let your imagination run wild.

Makes about 25 bars

1 cup granulated sugar
1/3 cup unsalted butter, melted
   and cooled
2 eggs
3/4 cup all-purpose flour
1/4 cup unsweetened cocoa
   powder
1/2 teaspoon baking powder

1/2 teaspoon salt
1 cup pitted, chopped dates or
   prunes; chopped, dried figs or
   apricots; or raisins
1/2 cup chopped walnuts,
   pecans, hazelnuts, peanuts, or
   almonds
1 teaspoon vanilla

In a medium bowl with an electric mixer on medium speed, beat sugar, melted butter and eggs until well blended. Combine flour, cocoa powder, baking powder and salt; sift over egg mixture. Beat until well blended. Add dried fruit, nuts and vanilla. Stir with wooden spoon until well mixed. Spread mixture evenly in a greased 9x9x2-inch baking pan.

Bake in a preheated 350-degree oven 25 to 30 minutes. Let cool completely in pan on wire rack. Cut into squares; remove from pan.

Gooey Blondies

Narcisse S. Cadgène
Free-lance Writer, New York City, New York

If your kids would rather eat the batter than the finished product, these cookie bars are for them: All the gooey goodness of batter without the stomachaches later. And these cookies are so quick to prepare, even the fastest kids won't get to the batter before it's baked. Don't bother testing for doneness with a toothpick, they will always be gooey in the center!

Makes 28 bars

1/2 cup butter
1 box (16 ounces) dark brown sugar (about 2-1/2 cups)
2 eggs
1 teaspoon vanilla
1 cup all-purpose flour
1/2 teaspoon salt
1 cup coarsely chopped walnuts

Combine butter and brown sugar in saucepan. Cook over medium heat, stirring constantly, until bubbly. Let cool.

Transfer cooled butter mixture to a mixing bowl. With an electric mixer, beat in eggs and vanilla. Quickly stir in flour, salt and walnuts.

Pour batter into a greased 13x9x2-inch baking pan.

Bake in a preheated 325-degree oven about 35 minutes, or until the edges begin to brown slightly. Let cool before cutting.

Hazelnut Shortbread

Laura J. Barton
Free-lance Writer, Portland, Oregon

I have always loved the melt-in-the-mouth richness of shortbread, and used to make traditional shortbread frequently. Because I now live in the Northwest, I have been influenced by the availability of Oregon hazelnuts and now make hazelnut shortbread, which is a favorite after-dinner accompaniment to coffee.

Makes about 3 dozen cookies

1 cup butter, softened
3/4 cup sifted confectioners' sugar
1-1/2 teaspoons grated orange peel

1/2 teaspoon vanilla
2 cups all-purpose flour
1 cup ground hazelnuts (filberts)

In a medium bowl with an electric mixer, beat butter and sugar until fluffy. Add orange peel and vanilla; mix well. Stir in flour and hazelnuts, mixing to blend thoroughly.

Press dough evenly into a 15x10x1-inch jelly-roll pan. Bake in a preheated 325-degree oven 25 to 30 minutes, or just until shortbread begins to brown. Cut into 2-inch squares while warm. Remove from pan and let cool completely on wire racks. Store in airtight containers.

Iced Applesauce Bars

Rita Barrett

Vice President, International Cookbook Services, White Plains, New York

My mother used to make these wonderful cookies from scratch. She even made her own applesauce. Mother gave me the recipe so I could make them for my children. I didn't have much time to bake when my children were little, so I decided to see if I could find an acceptable short cut. Much to my delight, I got excellent results using a gingerbread mix and store-bought applesauce. Best of all, my mother still thinks I make her Applesauce Bars from scratch!

Makes 40 bars

1 package (14 ounces) gingerbread mix	1 cup raisins
3/4 cup applesauce	2 teaspoons grated lemon peel

Icing:

1-1/2 cups confectioners' sugar, sifted	1 to 2 tablespoons milk
	1 to 2 teaspoons lemon juice

In a medium mixing bowl with an electric mixer on high speed, beat dry gingerbread mix and applesauce 2 minutes. Add raisins and lemon peel; stir to combine. Spread mixture evenly in greased and floured 13x9x2-inch baking pan.

Bake in a preheated 350-degree oven 25 to 30 minutes, or until center springs back when lightly pressed. Let cool completely in pan on wire rack.

For Icing: Blend confectioners' sugar, milk and lemon juice in a small bowl, stirring until smooth. Drizzle icing over baked layer in pan; let stand until icing is set.

Cut into bars. Remove bars from pan and store in cookie tins or airtight containers to enhance flavor.

Just Brownies

Toni Burks

Food Editor, *Roanoke Times & World-News*, Roanoke, Virginia

This is the first "cookie" I learned to make, the first "cookie" that I taught my daughter to make, the only "cookie" my husband knows how to make, and THE recipe I've shared with singles when they have someone special to impress. And it's just brownies, with a few refinements over fortysomething years.

Makes 16 brownies

1/2 cup butter
3 squares (1 ounce each) unsweetened chocolate
1 cup granulated sugar
2 eggs

1 teaspoon vanilla
3/4 cup sifted all-purpose flour
1-1/2 cups chopped walnuts, divided

Fudge Frosting:
1/2 of a 1-ounce square unsweetened chocolate
1 tablespoon butter

2 tablespoons milk
3/4 cup sifted confectioners' sugar

Combine butter and chocolate in medium saucepan; heat over medium heat, stirring frequently, until melted. Remove from heat.

Stir in sugar, using a wooden spoon to mix well. Blend in eggs, one at a time. Add vanilla; mix well. Stir in flour and 1 cup walnuts; mix well.

Spread batter in a greased 8x8x2-inch baking pan. Bake in a preheated 350-degree oven exactly 25 minutes. Do not overbake; brownies should be fudgey. Remove from oven and place pan on wire rack to cool completely.

For Fudge Frosting: In a small saucepan over very low heat, combine chocolate, butter and milk. Heat, stirring constantly, until chocolate and butter are melted. Beat in confectioners' sugar. Mix well.

Spread Fudge Frosting on cooled brownies in pan. Sprinkle remaining 1/2 cup chopped walnuts on top. Cut into squares.

Knock You Nakeds

Doris Reynolds

Food Columnist, *Naples Daily News*, Naples, Florida

A reader of my column requested a recipe for a dessert she ate at a food festival. She did not believe it when someone told her it was called Knock You Nakeds. I found the recipe in a cookbook called Great Flavors of Mississippi. *After I published it, several readers wrote to tell me that the recipe, under the name Chocolate Caramel Squares, had been a winner of a Pillsbury Bake-Off. This has been the most requested recipe I have ever printed. I have made it myself many times and there is never a crumb left. This is the most irresistible recipe I have ever published, prepared or eaten.*

Makes 16 to 20 bars

1 package (18-1/2 ounces) German chocolate cake mix
1 cup chopped pecans
1/3 cup plus 1/2 cup evaporated milk, divided

3/4 cup butter, melted
60 vanilla caramels, unwrapped (one 14 ounce package)
1 cup semisweet chocolate morsels

In a large mixing bowl, combine dry cake mix, pecans, 1/3 cup evaporated milk and melted butter. Press half of the batter into the bottom of a greased 13x9x2-inch glass baking dish. Bake in a preheated 350-degree oven 8 minutes.

In the top of a double boiler over simmering water, melt caramels with remaining 1/2 cup evaporated milk. When caramel mixture is well mixed, pour over baked layer. Cover with chocolate morsels. Pour remaining batter on top of morsels. Return to preheated 350-degree oven and bake 18 minutes. Let cool before cutting into squares.

Lemon Streusel Squares

Marlene Sorosky
Free-lance Writer, Hunt Valley, Maryland

My German grandmother, Oma, was a great baker. She was famous in our neighborhood for her fabulous butter cookies, which became the base for every cookie she ever made. This recipe is one I've adapted from her basic dough. Although she made the pastry by hand, I assemble it, as well as the filling, in the food processor. The buttery walnut-studded pastry plays a dual role — it is the base and streusel-like topping enveloping a wonderfully tangy lemon custard.

Makes 25 squares

Walnut Lemon Pastry:
2 medium lemons
1/3 cup granulated sugar
1 cup walnuts

1/2 cup unsalted butter or margarine, cold and cut into 8 pieces
3/4 cup all-purpose flour

Lemon Filling:
4 eggs
3/4 cup granulated sugar
1/4 cup unsalted butter or margarine, melted

1/3 cup plus 1 tablespoon lemon juice
1-1/2 teaspoons all-purpose flour

Line an 8x8x2-inch or 9x9x2-inch baking pan with heavy foil, letting foil extend an inch over the sides; set pan aside.

To make the pastry, peel the lemons using a vegetable peeler, taking care to remove as little white as possible. Place the peel in bowl of a food processor fitted with the metal blade; process until finely chopped. Add sugar and process until peel is minced. Add walnuts; pulse to a medium chop. Remove 1/2 cup of this mixture for the topping and set aside. Add butter and flour to mixture remaining in the work bowl; pulse until the mixture begins to hold together. Turn pastry into the prepared pan and press evenly into bottom of pan.

Bake in the center of a preheated 350-degree oven 20 to 24 minutes, or until the edges are golden and the top is set and very lightly colored.

Meanwhile, make the filling. In the same food processor bowl, mix eggs, sugar, butter, lemon juice and flour until blended. Pour filling over baked crust. Return to 350-degree oven and bake 10 to 12 minutes, or until filling is barely set.

Crumble reserved 1/2 cup walnut-lemon mixture; sprinkle over filling. Return to 350-degree oven and bake 8 to 10 minutes, or until filling is set. Let cool to room temperature.

Remove from pan by lifting out the foil; place on cutting board. Trim edges and cut into squares. The squares can be refrigerated for several days or frozen. Serve chilled or at room temperature.

Meringue Bars

Laura J. Barton
Free-lance Writer, Portland, Oregon

I was introduced to hazelnuts while living in Europe. Now that I live in Oregon, where 98 percent of the U.S. hazelnut crop is grown, my file of hazelnut recipes continues to grow. The following is a favorite; it is often requested by my family.

Makes about 30 bars

1/2 cup butter
1/2 cup sifted confectioners' sugar
2 eggs, separated
1 cup sifted all-purpose flour

1/2 cup granulated sugar
1/2 teaspoon ground cinnamon
1 cup ground, toasted hazelnuts (filberts)

Mix together thoroughly the butter, confectioners' sugar, egg yolks and flour. Press mixture into the bottom of a 13x9x2-inch baking pan. Bake in a preheated 350-degree oven 10 minutes.

While the crust is baking, beat egg whites until stiff. Gradually beat in granulated sugar and cinnamon. Fold in ground hazelnuts.

Spread egg white mixture over the partly baked crust. Return to 350-degree oven and bake 25 minutes, or until the topping is golden brown. Let cool slightly, then cut into bars. Store in airtight containers.

Mint-Chocolate Frosted Brownies

Patricia G. Gray
News Assistant, *The Express,* Easton, Pennsylvania

Because members of my family have a weakness for brownies, mint and chocolate, it made sense to combine all three. The green mint layer adds the right color at Christmas time, but the brownies are welcome at birthday parties, reunions or showers. The mint layer can be varied by adding crushed peppermint candy and red food color.

Makes 32 brownies

Brownies:

5 squares (1 ounce each) unsweetened chocolate
3/4 cup butter or margarine
1 tablespoon vanilla
2-1/4 cups granulated sugar

4 eggs
1-1/3 cups all-purpose flour
1-1/2 cups coarsely chopped walnuts

Mint Layer:

4 cups confectioners' sugar
1 package (3 ounces) cream cheese, softened
1/4 cup butter or margarine, softened

3 tablespoons milk
1 teaspoon vanilla
1/4 teaspoon peppermint extract
6 drops green food color

Frosting:

1 package (6 ounces) semisweet chocolate morsels

3 tablespoons butter or margarine

For Brownies: In a small saucepan over low heat, melt chocolate and butter, stirring constantly. Remove from heat. Stir in vanilla. In a large bowl, beat sugar and eggs until sugar is dissolved. Fold chocolate mixture, flour and walnuts into egg mixture until blended. Pour batter into a greased 13x9x2-inch baking pan. Bake in a preheated 375-degree oven 25 to 35 minutes. Do not overbake. Let cool completely.

Meanwhile, prepare Mint Layer: In a large bowl, combine confectioners' sugar, cream cheese, butter, milk, vanilla, peppermint extract and green food color; mix well. Spread over cooled brownies in pan.

Then prepare Frosting: In a small saucepan over low heat, melt chocolate and butter, stirring frequently. Spoon frosting evenly over mint layer; spread it carefully to the edges. Refrigerate brownies until firm; cut into bars.

Orange Slice Bars

Barbara Mihalevich Arciero
Food Writer, *The Times,* Shreveport, Louisiana

If retirement didn't keep my mother so busy — and if someone would clean up after her — she'd probably spend half her days in the kitchen. She loves to try new recipes. This cookie recipe is one my mother, Cheryl Goodnight of Shelbina, Missouri, spotted a good 30 or 40 years ago in a women's magazine. It's still a favorite.

Makes about 4-1/2 dozen cookies

1 pound candy orange slices,
cut into small pieces
2 cups sifted all-purpose flour
1/2 teaspoon salt
3 cups firmly packed brown
sugar

1 teaspoon vanilla
4 eggs, slightly beaten
1 cup chopped pecans
Granulated sugar (optional)

In a large mixing bowl, combine cut-up orange slices, flour and salt; toss to dredge orange slices with flour. Add brown sugar, vanilla, eggs and pecans; mix well with a spoon. Divide batter between 2 greased 9x9x2-inch pans.

Bake in a preheated 350-degree oven about 45 minutes. Let cool in pans, then cut into bars. Roll bars in granulated sugar, if desired.

Peanut Bars

Toni Burks

Food Editor, *Roanoke Times & World-News*, Roanoke, Virginia

*If you're partial to the homeyness of peanut butter
cookies, then you'll find a place in your heart for these
peanut bars. They get their good flavor from chopped
peanuts, not peanut butter. And the frosting—certainly
with chocolate lovers in mind—couldn't be easier. Just
sprinkle chocolate chips over the hot-from-the-oven
cookies, let stand for a bit, then spread.*

Makes 6 dozen bars

1-1/4 cups butter, softened, divided

1 cup firmly packed light brown sugar

1 teaspoon plus 1-1/2 tablespoons vanilla, divided

2 cups all-purpose flour

2 cans (14 ounces each) sweetened condensed milk (not evaporated milk)

1/2 teaspoon salt

2 cups finely chopped cocktail peanuts, divided

1 package (6 ounces) semisweet chocolate morsels

In a large mixing bowl with an electric mixer, beat 1 cup butter until light and fluffy. Add brown sugar and 1 teaspoon vanilla. Beat until well mixed. Blend in flour. Pat mixture evenly into a 15x10x1-inch jelly-roll pan, extending half way up sides. Bake in a preheated 350-degree oven 15 minutes.

Meanwhile, in medium saucepan, combine sweetened condensed milk, remaining 1/4 cup butter, remaining 1-1/2 tablespoons vanilla and salt. Heat over low heat, stirring occasionally, until butter melts. Increase temperature to medium-low and cook, stirring frequently and watching carefully (mixture has a tendency to scorch if heat is too high), until thickened. Stir in 1 cup peanuts.

Pour mixture over partly baked crust. Return to 350-degree oven and bake 15 minutes, or until lightly browned and set.

Remove from oven and immediately sprinkle chocolate morsels over top. Set aside until chocolate has softened sufficiently to spread it evenly over top. Sprinkle with remaining 1 cup peanuts. Let cool completely, then cut into bars.

Note: These bar cookies freeze well.

Peanut Butter Brownies

Clara Eschmann
Food Columnist, *Macon Telegraph & News*, Macon, Georgia

As a loyal Georgian, I love recipes that contain peanuts because peanuts are our state's biggest cash crop. Aside from that, my entire family has always liked peanuts in any shape or form. They are high in protein, full of B-complex vitamins and have no cholesterol — all points in their favor. I constantly try out new recipes using peanuts or peanut butter. The following is one that was given to me by a friend who knows about my enthusiasm for peanuts in any shape or form! My entire family likes this recipe.

Makes 2 dozen (2-inch) brownies

1/2 cup sifted all-purpose flour
1/4 teaspoon salt
1/2 cup crunchy peanut butter
1/4 cup butter or margarine
1 teaspoon vanilla

1 cup firmly packed brown
  sugar
2 eggs, unbeaten
1 cup chopped roasted peanuts

Combine flour and salt. Set aside. In a mixing bowl with an electric mixer, beat together peanut butter, butter and vanilla. Add brown sugar gradually, beating until well blended. Add eggs, one at a time, beating well after each addition. Blend in reserved flour mixture, then stir in peanuts; mix well. Spoon batter into a greased 8x8x2-inch baking pan. Spread evenly.

Bake in a preheated 350-degree oven 30 to 35 minutes, or until center is firm. Let cool in pan for 5 minutes before cutting into squares of desired size.

Peanut Butter and Jelly Bars

Norma Schonwetter
Syndicated Food Columnist, Oak Park, Michigan

Here's a cookie reminiscent of the popular peanut butter and jelly sandwich. A reader sent it to me asking me how she could make it in the microwave oven and requesting that it be cholesterol free. I substituted egg whites for the eggs, which eliminated the cholesterol. My samplers were adults and children. To my surprise, the adults liked them as much as the children.

Makes 2 dozen bars

3 cups all-purpose flour
1 cup granulated sugar
1-1/2 teaspoons baking powder
1/2 cup margarine, softened

1/2 cup chunky peanut butter
2 egg whites, slightly beaten
1 cup grape jelly

Combine flour, sugar and baking powder in large bowl. Cut in margarine and peanut butter until mixture resembles coarse meal. Stir in egg whites, mixing well until flour is moistened.

Press half of the dough into a greased 13x9x2-inch baking pan. Spread grape jelly over dough. Crumble remaining half of dough over jelly.

Bake in a preheated 375-degree oven 30 to 35 minutes, or until crumbs are firm and dry. Let cool, then cut into bars.

Note: These cookies freeze well.

Pear Treasure Squares

Kathleen Stang
Free-lance Food Writer, Seattle, Washington

I adapted this recipe from one provided by the canned pear industry. Canned pears are convenient and contribute to the keeping quality of these moist cookies. Choose your favorite "treasures" according to what you have on hand. The recipe is fast and easy enough for kids to make.

Makes 2 dozen bars

1 can (16 ounces) pears in natural juices
1/2 cup butter or margarine, softened
3/4 cup firmly packed brown sugar
1 egg
1 teaspoon vanilla
1-3/4 cups whole wheat flour
1 teaspoon baking soda
1/2 teaspoon salt

1/2 teaspoon ground cinnamon
3 cups "treasures" such as:
1-1/2 cups miniature semisweet chocolate morsels or butterscotch morsels;
1 cup golden raisins, dark raisins or pitted chopped dates;
1/2 cup chopped hazelnuts (filberts), walnuts or pecans

Drain pears, reserving 1/2 cup liquid; dice pears.

In a large mixing bowl with an electric mixer, beat butter and brown sugar until fluffy. Add egg, vanilla and reserved 1/2 cup pear liquid; mix well. Combine flour, baking soda, salt and cinnamon; stir into butter mixture along with "treasures" and diced pears.

Spray a 13x9x2-inch baking pan with non-stick cooking spray. Turn batter into pan. Bake in a preheated 350-degree oven 30 to 35 minutes, or until wooden pick inserted near center comes out clean. Cut into bars while still warm.

Pecan Pie Squares

Anne Byrn

Food Writer, *Atlanta Journal-Constitution*, Atlanta, Georgia

Nothing is more Southern than pecan pie. What better way to make the taste of the South portable than to bake the confection in a rectangular baking pan and cut it into squares? These invariably pop up at brunches and picnics because they are simple to prepare and taste so good. Chocoholics can scatter one package (12 ounces) semisweet chocolate morsels on top of the hot, baked layer and swirl the melted chocolate to create an icing.

Makes about 2 dozen squares

Crust:

2 cups sifted all-purpose flour	1/2 teaspoon salt
1/4 cup granulated sugar	1/2 cup unsalted butter, melted

Filling:

3 eggs, lightly beaten	2 tablespoons butter, melted
1 cup granulated sugar	1 teaspoon vanilla
1 cup light corn syrup	2 cups chopped pecans

For Crust: In a large mixing bowl, combine flour, sugar, salt and butter. Mix on medium speed of electric mixer until mixture resembles coarse meal. (This also can be done in a food processor.) Press crust mixture firmly into a greased 13x9x2-inch baking pan. Bake in a preheated 350-degree oven 20 minutes, or until golden brown.

For Filling: In a mixing bowl, combine eggs, sugar, corn syrup, butter, vanilla and pecans.

Pour filling over baked crust. Return to 350-degree oven and bake 25 to 30 minutes, or until filling is just set. Let cool before cutting into squares.

Pecan Prune Bars

Lori Longbotham,
Food Columnist, *New York Post*, New York, New York

There's a lot of fiber in these delicious prune bars—in the bran, the oatmeal, and the prunes; but they don't taste healthful, they taste delectable. These cookies can be served anytime of the day—to young and old. They are a wonderful lunch box treat, a sophisticated teatime nibble, great for dessert, or a healthful snack anytime. These are best if they sit for 24 hours before cutting.

Makes 3-1/2 dozen cookies

3 extra-large eggs or equivalent egg substitute
1 cup honey
1 teaspoon vanilla
1 cup all-purpose flour
1/2 cup old-fashioned rolled oats, uncooked
1/2 cup rice bran or oat bran
1 teaspoon baking powder
1/2 teaspoon ground cinnamon
1/4 teaspoon ground cloves
1/4 teaspoon salt
12 ounces pitted prunes, coarsely chopped
1 cup chopped pecans
Confectioners' sugar

In a large bowl with an electric mixer on high speed, beat eggs about 4 minutes, or until light and lemon colored. Gradually add honey and vanilla, beating constantly.

Combine flour, oats, bran, baking powder, cinnamon, cloves and salt. Gradually stir flour mixture into egg mixture with a rubber spatula just until blended. Fold in prunes and pecans, mixing thoroughly.

Pour batter into a well-oiled 13x9x2-inch baking pan. Smooth top. Bake in a preheated 350-degree oven about 40 minutes, or until lightly browned and springy to the touch. Do not overbake.

Let cool in pan on a wire rack, then cut into bars. Roll each bar in confectioners' sugar before serving.

Pumpkin Bars

Doris Reynolds
Food Columnist, *Naples Daily News*, Naples, Florida

At Halloween, I try to print some recipes using pumpkin. One year I had a request from a reader who wanted a recipe for pumpkin cookies that she could freeze, because her family usually had a huge pumpkin and she was running out of ideas on how to use the pumpkin flesh. I tested this recipe from a cookbook called Orchard Fresh*, put out by the Essex County (Massachusetts) Fruit Growers Association. This recipe can be prepared with either fresh or canned pumpkin.*

Makes 20 cookies

4 eggs
1-2/3 cups granulated sugar
1 cup vegetable oil
2 cups cooked pumpkin or
   1 can (16 ounces) pumpkin

2 cups all-purpose flour
2 teaspoons baking powder
2 teaspoons ground cinnamon
1 teaspoon salt

Cream Cheese Frosting:
1 package (3 ounces) cream
   cheese, softened
1/2 cup butter

1 teaspoon vanilla
2 cups confectioners' sugar

In a mixing bowl, beat eggs with a fork. Add sugar, oil, pumpkin, flour, baking powder, cinnamon and salt; mix well. Pour batter into greased 13x9x2-inch baking pan. Bake in a preheated 350-degree oven 25 to 30 minutes. Do not overbake. Let cool in pan.

For Cream Cheese Frosting: In a mixing bowl, combine cream cheese, butter, vanilla and confectioners' sugar. Beat until smooth.

Frost cooled cookie layer (still in pan) with cream cheese frosting. Cut into bars. Store in refrigerator. These freeze beautifully.

Spotted Blondies

Frances Price
Food Columnist, Baltimore, Maryland

White chocolate is quite fashionable right now, but it isn't really chocolate because it's made without cocoa butter. True chocolate lovers find its flavor a blanched imitation of deep, dark chocolate. To compensate for that lack, I've boosted flavor in this stylish blonde version of brownies with chocolate morsels, which are decorative as well as delicious.

Makes 25 brownies

1/2 cup butter
6 squares (1 ounce each) white chocolate
2 eggs
2/3 cup granulated sugar
2 teaspoons grated orange peel or 1 teaspoon vanilla

1-1/2 cups all-purpose flour
1/2 teaspoon baking powder
1/2 cup semisweet chocolate morsels

Melt butter; set aside. Melt white chocolate according to package directions; set aside.

In a large mixing bowl, beat eggs by hand until foamy. Stir in sugar and orange peel. Add melted butter and melted white chocolate.

Sift flour with baking powder. Blend flour mixture into egg mixture. Stir in chocolate morsels. Spread batter evenly in a greased 9x9x2-inch baking pan. Bake in a preheated 350-degree oven 25 to 30 minutes, or until top is dull and set. Let cool in pan on rack 15 to 30 minutes, then cut into squares.

Strawberry Cheesecake Squares

Jean Rogers

Food Editor, *Prevention Magazine*, Emmaus, Pennsylvania

These easy cheesecake squares have a creamy, fruit-flavored filling. The recipe is adapted from one that appears in my book, Cooking with the Healthful Herbs *(Rodale Press, 1983). You can make these squares as healthful or rich as you desire by varying the main ingredients. I've found the recipe works just fine using light margarine, Neufchatel cheese and fat-free egg substitute in place of butter, cream cheese and eggs. You also can vary the fruit, using chopped peeled peaches or other summer fruit.*

Makes 16 squares

Crust:

1/2 cup coarsely chopped walnuts or pecans

1 cup all-purpose flour

1/3 cup firmly packed light brown sugar

5 tablespoons light margarine or unsalted butter

Filling:

1 package (8 ounces) Neufchatel cheese or cream cheese

1/3 cup firmly packed light brown sugar

2 cups sliced strawberries

1/2 cup fat-free egg substitute or 2 eggs

1 tablespoon lemon juice

1 teaspoon vanilla

For Crust: Place nuts in the bowl of a food processor fitted with a steel blade. Process with a few on/off turns until nuts are finely chopped. Add flour and brown sugar to the bowl. Cut margarine into 1/2-inch pieces and add to the bowl. Process with on/off turns until the mixture resembles coarse meal.

Reserve 1 cup crumb mixture. Press remaining crumb mixture firmly and evenly into an ungreased 8x8x2-inch baking dish. Bake in the middle of a preheated 350-degree oven 10 minutes, or until lightly browned. Remove from oven.

For Filling: While the crust is baking, cut Neufchatel cheese into cubes and place in food processor work bowl (no need to wash it out first). Crumble brown sugar into bowl to break up any lumps. Process about 15 seconds, or until well blended. Add strawberries; process 15 seconds, or until smooth. Add egg substitute, lemon juice and vanilla. Process 10 seconds, or until well combined.

Pour filling over hot crust. Sprinkle with reserved 1 cup crumb mixture.

Return to 350-degree oven and bake 30 to 40 minutes, or until the outside edges are puffed and a knife inserted in the center comes out fairly clean.

Let cool on a wire rack, then refrigerate until thoroughly chilled before cutting into squares.

Toffee Bars

Ann Corell Wells
Food Editor, *The Grand Rapids Press,* Grand Rapids, Michigan

Better than candy, these toffee bar cookies have only two drawbacks — they're so tasty they don't last long enough to get them out of the pan, and if they do last, they must be refrigerated. I never have enough room in the refrigerator for keeping cookies, so they must be eaten right away. The recipe was given to me several years ago by the entertainment editor at our paper who often made them as a treat for the office.

Makes 3 dozen bars, depending on size

1 cup butter (not margarine)	1 teaspoon vanilla
1 cup firmly packed brown sugar	1 package (12 ounces) semisweet chocolate morsels
1 egg yolk	1 to 1-1/2 cups chopped walnuts
2 cups all-purpose flour	

In a large bowl with an electric mixer, beat butter and brown sugar until fluffy. Mix in egg yolk, flour and vanilla. Spread dough into a 15x10x1-inch jelly-roll pan and pat to about 1/4-inch thickness. Bake in a preheated 350-degree oven 15 minutes.

Remove from oven. While still hot, sprinkle chocolate morsels on top. With table knife, spread melting chocolate to cover surface. Sprinkle walnuts over chocolate. Cut into bars while still warm.

Note: These cookies freeze well. Layer bars in a rigid container with waxed paper or foil between layers.

29 Palms Date Bars

Laura J. Barton
Free-lance Writer, Portland, Oregon

I usually make bar cookies because they are so quick. The following recipe was developed during an on-location project in the Southern California desert, where a fully stocked kitchen was not available. The ingredients on hand led to tasty results. This has become part of my cookie repertoire.

Makes about 16 cookies

1-1/2 cups pitted, chopped dates
1 cup lemonade (homemade or from a mix)
1/4 cup granulated sugar
1/2 cup chopped, unblanched almonds
1-1/2 cups all-purpose flour
1-1/2 cups quick-cooking rolled oats, uncooked
1/2 cup firmly packed brown sugar
1/4 teaspoon salt
3/4 cup butter

In a small saucepan, combine dates, lemonade and sugar. Cook over high heat until boiling. Reduce heat to low; simmer 5 minutes, or until mixture thickens. Remove from heat; stir in almonds.

In a medium mixing bowl, combine flour, oats, brown sugar and salt. Cut in butter until mixture resembles coarse crumbs.

Pat half of the oats mixture into a 9x9x2-inch baking pan. Spread the date mixture over oats mixture in pan, then top with the remaining oats mixture. Bake in a preheated 375-degree oven 30 minutes, or until done. Let cool in pan, then cut into bars.

The Ultimate Brownie

Carolyn Flournoy
Cooking Columnist, *The Times,* Shreveport, Louisiana

This is a Texas version of the "ultimate" creation with a Louisiana twist. A friend got it from a haute cuisine Houston hostess and gave it to me after making me promise I would never reveal it. That was nine years ago and I believe the statute of limitations has run out. Enjoy!

Makes about 3 dozen brownies

2 ounces dark unsweetened chocolate
1/2 cup butter
1/2 cup semisweet chocolate morsels
2 eggs

1 cup granulated sugar
1/2 teaspoon vanilla
1/2 cup all-purpose flour
2/3 cup broken pecans
1 cup miniature marshmallows

In the top of a double boiler over simmering water, melt dark chocolate, butter and semisweet chocolate morsels. Stir to mix.

In a large mixing bowl, beat eggs, sugar and vanilla. Stir in flour and the chocolate mixture. Add pecans and marshmallows. Pour mixture into a heavily buttered 8x8x2-inch baking pan. Bake in a preheated 350-degree oven 20 to 25 minutes. Let cool, then cut into squares.

Index